Praise for
Men Who Love Fierce Women

He's quiet, she's "fierce." The more she pushes, the more he withdraws. The less he leads, the more she takes over. If this sounds familiar—and if you're tired of the cycle—LeRoy and Kimberly Wagner have the answer. They'll show how you can learn to work together as a team, channeling personality differences for *constructive* rather than *destructive* purposes.

JIM DALY
President, Focus on the Family

Being married to a strong person is something we both understand. This kind of marriage partnership presents unique challenges, but it also promises wonderful opportunities. We are deeply grateful to our friends, LeRoy and Kim, for writing such a helpful, biblically grounded book, born out of their personal journey and the transformation God has brought about in their lives. We strongly commend this book to you as God continues to write His story in and through your life and marriage.

ROBERT & NANCY (DeMoss) WOLGEMUTH

In this book, LeRoy and Kim help us understand how marital conflict can either destroy a marriage or be the means God uses to develop qualities of leadership, communication, and intimacy. Here is practical guidance for men to step to the plate and realize that leading a strong wife is not impossible. Instead, it can be a journey that leads to mutual fulfillment, spirited growth, and genuine appreciation for one another. We will personally profit from the wisdom and hard truth found in these pages.

ERWIN & REBECCA LUTZER
Pastor Emeritus, The Moody Church

I have known LeRoy and Kim as friends since college. They are real, they are transparent, they love God, and they love you. If you are tired of marriage books that present an idyllic, stereotypical, "everyone fits in the exact same box" approach, then you will love this book. Thank you, LeRoy and Kim, for ministering to those of us who come away from most marriage conferences feeling worse than we did before!

J.D. "SONNY" TUCKER
Executive Director, Arkansas Baptist State Convention

Talk about a captivating book! The Wagners' description of "Courageous Leaders verses Passive Deserters" is worth the price of the book. You will pass this marriage book along to others.

JOHNNY M. HUNT
Senior Pastor, FBC Woodstock
Former SBC President

This book was hard to read for me because I am a fierce woman, but this has helped me see how my fierceness made my husband feel. I have cried several times as I read, and it has given me opportunities to go to Wade and seek forgiveness—which is always a good place for me to be. Thank you for taking the time and effort (I know it can't be easy) to write this hard, but necessary book.

BECKY ARNOLD
Wife, mom, and follower of Jesus Christ

With uncommon honesty, LeRoy and Kim provide us a raw account of how a spiral into marital-induced depression can become fuel for great hope! They are walking reminders that the cycle of pain can be broken and a marriage revolution for God's glory is possible with Christ!

BYRON PAULUS
President/Executive Director, Life Action Ministries

The words that come to mind when I think of this amazing couple and their story of a redeemed marriage are biblical, transparent, courageous, and compassionate. Gratefully, LeRoy has now transferred this personal story into the principles of this book for these very same words to ring true in the hearts of husbands and homes.

PAUL H. JIMENEZ
Senior Pastor, Taylors First Baptist Church, Taylors, SC

Kimberly Wagner's *Fierce Women* was so impactful for the women of our church but one of the main questions we heard was, "Why can't there be a book like *Fierce Women* for our husbands, so they can grow in these areas as well?" *Men Who Love Fierce Women* is the book that we were waiting for. In it, LeRoy and Kimberly Wagner serve as faithful guides who take us on a journey through both Scripture and their personal struggles in order to equip us with practical help to find our way back to God's design for marriage.

JUAN & JEANINE SANCHEZ
High Pointe Baptist Church, Austin, TX

It isn't surprising in today's culture that there are many husbands married to strong, fierce women who are simply checking out emotionally. LeRoy and Kim's willingness to be transparent and open about what they experienced in their marriage has already helped countless couples. This is a book that will bring real help—and healing—to both husbands and wives.

BOB & MARY ANN LEPINE
Co-host, FamilyLife Today

THE POWER OF SERVANT
LEADERSHIP IN YOUR MARRIAGE

Men Who Love
Fierce Women

LEROY & KIMBERLY WAGNER

MOODY PUBLISHERS
CHICAGO

Unless otherwise noted, Scripture quotations are from *The Holy Bible, English Standard Version*® (ESV), copyright © 2001, 2007 by Crossway, a publishing ministry of Good News Publishers. Used by permission. All rights reserved.

Scripture quotations marked NASB are taken from the *New American Standard Bible*®, Copyright © 1960, 1962, 1963, 1968, 1971, 1972, 1973, 1975, 1977, 1995 by The Lockman Foundation. Used by permission. (www.Lockman.org)

Scripture quotations marked NIV are taken from the Holy Bible, New International Version®, NIV®. Copyright © 1973, 1978, 1984, 2011 by Biblica, Inc.™ Used by permission of Zondervan. All rights reserved worldwide. www.zondervan.com. The "NIV" and "New International Version" are trademarks registered in the United States Patent and Trademark Office by Biblica, Inc.™

Scripture quotations marked KJV are taken from the King James Version

Edited by Elizabeth Cody Newenhuyse
Interior design: Smartt Guys design
Cover design: Connie Gabbert Design and Illustration
Cover photo: Natalie Puls (nataliepuls.com)
Author photo: Lindsey Landrum Photography

Library of Congress Cataloging-in-Publication Data

Names: Wagner, LeRoy, author.
Title: Men who love fierce women : the power of servant leadership in your
  marriage / LeRoy and Kimberly Wagner.
Description: Chicago : Moody Publishers, 2016. | Includes bibliographical
  references.
Identifiers: LCCN 2016024411 (print) | LCCN 2016027119 (ebook) | ISBN
  9780802414656 | ISBN 9780802494627 ()
Subjects: LCSH: Marriage--Religious aspects--Christianity. | Man-woman
  relationships--Religious aspects--Christianity. | Women--Psychology.
Classification: LCC BV835 .W3425 2016 (print) | LCC BV835 (ebook) | DDC
  248.8/425--dc23
LC record available at https://lccn.loc.gov/2016024411

ISBN: 978-0-8024-1465-6

We hope you enjoy this book from Moody Publishers. Our goal is to provide high-quality, thought-provoking books and products that connect truth to your real needs and challenges. For more information on other books and products written and produced from a biblical perspective, go to www.moodypublishers.com or write to:

Moody Publishers
820 N. LaSalle Boulevard
Chicago, IL 60610

3 5 7 9 10 8 6 4 2

Printed in the United States of America

We owe our marriage rescue to God's grace,
but we are eternally grateful for a dear friend that He used
as the vital instrument in that grace operation.
Thank you for coming alongside a brokenhearted fierce wife,
and challenging her to consider whether she might
intimidate her husband!
Thank you for being the truth-speaking friend and confidante
that walked alongside us in God's recovery process.
We are eternally indebted to you, and dedicate this book to you
as fruit of your labor in our lives, Nancy DeMoss Wolgemuth.

Contents

This book contains stories of many hurting couples
we've counseled in more than three decades of ministry.
We've changed the names in most cases as well as some details,
because many of these accounts could carry several names.
The sad, but true, fact is that marriages within the church
are broken and needy. And many husbands have lost all hope.
Although we may not know you personally, you probably
can find your story here, bearing another name, but one
you can identify with in an uncomfortably personal way.
We are grateful to those courageous friends who
gave us permission to share their stories and we hope
that one day your story can be shared as well.

We pray that God will transform your life
and your marriage for His glory!

Why Should You Read This Book?

Whe were three days into the honeymoon when I knew we were in big trouble. Some marriage problems take years to form, but we were struggling from the beginning. You take one fierce woman, combine that with a non-confrontational "nice guy," and you have a recipe for disaster. At least that's what was happening in our marriage.

Five years in, and I was pretty much done. We weren't planning to divorce, but just settled into a routine of living like unfriendly roommates and existing in a holding pattern of "ceasefire" between enemies. We entered a long period of misery and hopelessness.

Can you relate?

We were searching for answers, but kept coming back empty-handed. I tried to be a good husband, to please my wife, to do what was right, but it never seemed good enough. She was miserable. I was miserable. And we were stuck.

We were stuck in a destructive relationship pattern that we call the "Fierce Woman/Fearful Man" cycle. It was sheer torment. But what we thought would destroy us actually became what brought us to a deeper understanding of God's love.

This book tells our story. We've been amazed by what God has done and frankly, it is embarrassing to share with you all the raw and shameful journey of our marriage, but we have to. If our story can help, we're willing to tell it. We don't want you to keep groping for answers and coming up empty. And we want you to understand just how amazing God is and what He can do.

Through this book, and my wife's book, *Fierce Women: The Power of a Soft Warrior*, we're reaching out to couples who are in that painful place, where we were stuck for almost two decades, and sharing what God has taught us. He has completely transformed our relationship. We actually enjoy each other—and would never have imagined how good loving one another could be.

We're holding out a rope of rescue and letting you know—there is a reason for hope. There is an answer. God sees what you are facing, He knows what you are dealing with, and He cares. You are not alone, and He hasn't abandoned you.

Your journey to a new beginning starts here.

The Courageous Leader Within

The bravest are surely those who have the clearest vision
of what is before them, glory and danger alike,
and yet notwithstanding, go out to meet it.

THUCYDIDES

When we were at the lowest point in our marriage, my wife would (not so subtly) pass on to me "helpful books." I wasn't a fan of those types of books. I enjoy reading, but I'd rather read just about anything than a book on "relationships." Maybe I shouldn't admit that in the first paragraph, but if I'm going to be honest with you throughout this process (and I am, I'll be painfully honest), then I might as well start by getting that confession out in the open.

So, knowing how I feel about "relationship books," why am I partnering with my wife to write a book on marriage?

If you're experiencing anything like we were for the first half of our marriage, then you're at a very dark place. You're struggling with feelings of failure, with a sense of worthlessness—feeling like no matter how hard you try, you can never do anything right. You've probably lost hope that things could ever improve in your relationship with your wife and you've resigned yourself to accepting the idea that this is how it's going to be for the rest of your life.

I want you to know that I'm here for you—that's why I'm writing this book. Because I've been to that place of hopelessness, stuck in a marital nightmare for several years, but I want you to know that there is reason for hope. There is a way out. The last half of our marriage bears proof of that. You can check out the video where we share some of our story here: http://www.kimberlywagner.org/?p=180.

But before we get too far into this, let's start by examining what it means to be a man. Any relationship we're involved in is affected by how we view manhood and how we relate to others as men. No matter what you hear the culture telling you today—manhood is not something to be ashamed of. Courageous manhood is what you and I were designed for.

What does it mean to be a man?

Answers abound on this one. Everybody seems to have an opinion.

Esquire has a few things to say on what makes a man:

A man carries cash. A man looks out for those around him—woman, friend, stranger. A man can cook eggs. A man can always find something good to watch on television. A man makes things—a rock wall, a table, the tuition money. Or he rebuilds—engines, watches, fortunes.

He passes along expertise, one man to the next. Know-how survives him . . . A man fantasizes that kung fu lives deep inside him somewhere . . . A man is good at his job. Not his work, not his avocation, not his hobby. Not his career. His job. It doesn't matter what his job is, because if a man doesn't like his job, he gets a new one.

A man can look you up and down and figure some things out. Before you say a word, he makes you. From your suitcase, from your watch, from your posture. A man infers.

A man owns up. That's why Mark McGwire is not a man. A man grasps his mistakes. He lays claim to who he is, and what he was, whether he likes them or not.

A man gets the door. Without thinking.

He stops traffic when he must.

A man is comfortable being alone. Loves being alone, actually. He sleeps.

Or he stands watch. He interrupts trouble. This is the state policeman. This is the poet. Men, both of them.

A man loves driving alone most of all.[1]

Esquire also reminds us that "Just being male doesn't make you a man." I would tweak *Esquire*'s description of manhood a bit, but on this point, they've got it right. Just being male doesn't make you a man; a man in the sense of living out your manhood as God created you to express it.

Manhood is under siege today and we're suffering the consequences of relinquishing it. Think back: When did you know you were a real man? How long has it been since you felt affirmed in your manhood?

When Fear Birthed a Man

At the skinny age of twelve, I was ready to prove myself as a man, ready for the initiation. But standing at the top of sheer bluffs, looking twenty feet below into the deep pool, the drop stretched much longer than what it looked at the water's surface. I was afraid, but resolute.

My assignment: survive the dive, push myself to reach the bottom, grab the rock of "proof" from the riverbed, and resurface before running out of oxygen. I knew what I faced, at least I thought I did, but looking down into the murky water below, I wasn't too sure. I'd tried this before, but every time the dive ended the same way:

THINK BACK: WHEN DID YOU KNOW YOU WERE A REAL MAN?

Epic failure.

I'd tried, but never been able to stay below the surface long enough to make it all the way to the bottom. The dive had to be near perfect for the initial plunge to send my boyish body as deep as possible. But today, no matter what, I had to do it. I had to make it to the bottom.

The innocent, lazy summer afternoon and the cheers of my buddies gave way to a colder, darker, and more sinister reality as I broke the water's surface and plunged beneath sunlight. Motivated by the challenge and the dread of failure (again), I kept pushing downward. But just like every other time, as the water's temperature grew frigid with depth, the blackness became disorienting and my lungs began their burn.

This was the point when I usually turned back.

This was the point when fear always kicked in.

At twelve, I wasn't completely free of night terrors and monsters that hid under the bed. In the darkness, my lack of fresh oxygen and disorientation grabbed hold of my boyish imagination. Fear was triggered big-time.

"If I make it to the bottom . . . what *will* I touch?"

Ignoring the burn, I pushed a little deeper. But as my outstretched hand groped for the elusive bottom, fear only increased.

Surely, I was too far to make it back to oxygen and sunshine. Who would pull my lifeless body from the water?

The temptation to turn back kicked in with greater intensity than I'd ever experienced. My lungs reached their limit, but I'd made my decision. I would reach the bottom dead or alive. No retreat this time! The moment I sealed that decision, my hand brushed something. Instinctively I recoiled, fearing the unknown and unfamiliar.

Did I touch bottom?

I reached out again and brushed the floor with my hand before grabbing a small rock. At the same time, I coiled my body and pushed hard against the rocky bottom with my feet to propel my body upward. Seconds later, I broke through the surface, gasping for air and gulping in mouthfuls of water, but holding my rock high above my head, while my buddies cheered.

They cheered because I conquered the river. But I knew that grabbing that rock signified more than pushing past burning lungs. The dive brought me face-to-face with my repeated failures and invited me to cave to fear again.

This time fear didn't win.

This time fear was conquered at the bottom.

This time fear birthed a "man."

My buddies celebrated the small victory, but were oblivious to its significance—the significance of learning one of the important lessons of manhood: courageously face your fears and push past the pain to conquer the prize.

All little boys see themselves as the hero in the battles fought in their minds, or the kingdoms they conquer on the playground. I cannot count how many times as a boy that I was up to bat, facing Catfish Hunter in the World Series, in the ninth inning, game tied, two outs. My hit over Reggie Jackson's head put the game away. I regularly shot baskets in my backyard after "weaving my way through a maze of defenders," fighting to make it to the backboard, my layup making the game-winning shot to bring home the victory to "my team." Personal victories fought and won in my adolescent mind encouraged me to defy the odds in real life.

Don't all men dream those dreams as boys?

Didn't you?

Maybe not now, but can you remember the time when you knew you could rise to the challenge? Defeat the fiercest enemy? Press into the pain, push the envelope, ignore the taunts, demonstrate skill, and embrace the agony?

Daring to do what you have never done before?

Manhood isn't born overnight, isn't dreamed into existence, but within every little boy lies the drive and desire to exert the strength, courage, skill, and knowledge that manhood requires. Manhood may be under siege today, but its DNA still flows through our veins. Its pulse may be faint, but it's there—you can't deny it.

What does it mean to be a man?

What is manhood?

It's been more than three millennia since that same question was asked by a real man's man, David—the warrior king of Israel. As a boy, not much older than I was when I took my dive to manhood in that frigid pool, David took down one of the nastiest enemies the armies of Israel had ever faced. So significant was his defeat of Goliath that women wrote songs about it. They danced in the streets while singing ballads of David's courageous victory (1 Samuel 18:6–8).

The ideal man that was praised for his courage to face the hairy Philistine giant (just guessing, surely he was hairy, lots of testosterone going on there), later penned this inquiry:

"What is man . . . ?"

Good question.

It's a question we men need to consider as we evaluate our place, our role, our purpose.

It's the question David asked when pondering the immense universe:

"When I look at your heavens, the work of your fingers, the moon and the stars, which you have set in place, what is man that you are mindful of him, and the son of man that you care for him?" (Psalm 8:3–4).

WHAT IS MAN?

What is man? Not in reference to other men, but in reference to "who is man" before God? Who is man, that God would be mindful of us—our lives, our condition, and our struggles? The fact that God would "be mindful of us" indicates that He had something in mind in creating us. Man was not created as a possibility to become something, but in the creative heart and mind of God, he was created with intention. God created man in such a way that we would reflect what He had in mind for us.

From the opening lines of Scripture, man is given an incredible designation that provides us with an understanding of our true worth and value as men. Only after heavenly bodies were put in place, paradise was prepared on earth, vegetation, plant, and animal life were set within an orderly structure, and all was deemed "good" by its Creator— only then, on the final day of creation, did the Master Designer take dirt in His hands to form one who would bear His image.

"Then the Lord God formed the man of dust from the ground and breathed into his nostrils the breath of life, and the man became a living creature. And the Lord God planted a garden in Eden, in the east, and there he put the man whom he had formed" (Genesis 2:7–8).

Man, the earthly reflection of God: man of dust—man of heaven.

Man's core identity and purpose are intimately tied to this event. Man was created to "image God." Adam's personality, work, daily schedule, (future) relationships, responsibilities, and very life, all flow from this distinction as God's image bearer. Man's role and assignments portray the character and ways of his Creator.

Working, managing the resources at hand, laboring, and producing, was Adam's commission from the very beginning, before the fall, before the eviction, before death entered creation. From the beginning, man's worth and value were not determined by his accomplishments, but by his identity as the image bearer. But as the image bearer, man was to apply himself to the noble pursuit of fruitful labor.

What was in the mind of God when He created the mind of man? Was man's assignment more than just tilling the earth and producing? The assignment to care for the garden implies the garden needed guidance in a certain direction, not left on its own. The animal kingdom needed its master to demonstrate his regency by naming each member. Creation needed Adam's management, oversight, and leadership.

> Now out of the ground the Lord God had formed every beast of the field and every bird of the heavens and brought them to the man to see what he would call them. And whatever the man called every living creature, that was its name. The man gave names to all livestock and to the birds of the heavens and to every beast of the field. But for Adam there was not found a helper fit for him. (Genesis 2:19–20)

God extended to man a measure of latitude and freedom to exercise his dominion and leadership over creation. God gave Adam the assignment to name the creatures as an exertion of his authority and headship over them. Creation was not to be left to its own.

This Is NOT Good

Man also was not to be left alone. In fact, that is where we see God's first declaration that something is "not good." The Genesis narrative, punctuating each divine act with affirmation of its goodness, is abruptly interrupted by this assessment—man's solo existence is deemed as "not good." Creation awaits completion.

Man, the first of his kind, regent over the world and all things in it, stands in need of his consort. Intelligent, productive, strong, in close relation with his God, but man waits, standing incomplete without his perfect complement. The divine Artisan moves to produce a most beautiful and excellent crowning jewel:

"Then the Lord God said, 'It is not good that the man should be alone; I will make him a helper fit for him'" (Genesis 2:18).

"Woman," according to Matthew Henry, "was made of a rib out of the side of Adam; not made out of his head to rule over him, nor out of his feet to be trampled upon by him, but out of his side to be equal with him, under his arm to be protected, and near his heart to be beloved."[2]

With woman, God brings creation to a state of perfection. All is now complete and assessed as "very good." Woman wasn't created as an afterthought; rather, she was part of His glorious plan from the beginning and His dramatic delay holds within it mysterious purpose.

Before sin, before the fall, God placed a longing in Adam's heart for something that was not found within all of the perfection of creation. God created a need within man that would only be completed by one thing that nothing else in all of creation could fulfill. God didn't observe a "loneliness" in Adam and then determine that he needed a mate. No, God planned the woman before the first molecule of earth was ever put in place, but in His wisdom, God refrained from giving man his perfect counterpart until man could be given opportunity to fully realize his need.

My Perfect Counterpart

The last bell for class was sounding. At its last note, she came flying through the door. Her dark hair swung across her shoulders and she seemed to take the fifteen steps from the door to her desk in one smooth stride. Her dramatic entry brought me out of my morning stupor and suddenly I was at full attention. That was my first encounter with the woman God had prepared for me. Something happened the moment I saw her. I felt it surge through my entire body—desire. Not a lustful desire, but a true desire that God put within man's DNA, the pure desire that finds its completion in the woman.

Adam's reaction to his perfect counterpart must have been similar to the surge I felt at the first glimpse of my future bride. After Adam spent time with the entire animal kingdom functioning in pairs, God pulled him aside to perform sacred surgery. God took from Adam, to give back to him that which he would be incomplete without. Man was the physical source God used in forming the woman. Eve was given life as an individual, but her original composition was designed from the man's own body. Think about it: Adam's body was broken sacrificially to provide the necessary physical components to produce his bride.

God had a perfect and noble purpose in creating woman from man. Woman is intimately connected with man as her fleshly source. The heart of fallen woman may seek to dominate man, but actually woman was created from and for man (1 Corinthians 11:9). And God saw that it was good, even *very good!*

Adam didn't have to pursue his bride: God brought her to him. God presents what is beyond Adam's wildest dreams, a woman, made for him, given to him, perfectly fulfilling the longing that God placed within his heart. Now, not only would Adam lead all of creation, but this one—his counterpart—was also entrusted to his leadership; the zenith of all creation, not formed from dust, but created from man.

This woman would serve as his coregent over creation.

God brought the first woman to the man. As a father bringing his daughter to the groom, God entrusted His gift to Adam. All things were created by Him and for Him—Jesus Christ Himself. The rescuer in the gospel story is here in this sacred ceremony uniting man and woman into one flesh; the first Adam and the second Adam were both participants in the wedding . . . the gospel portrayed.

What could possibly go wrong? It all seemed so right; all was so good. Perfect paradise.

Women Who Eat Men for Breakfast

The first conversation I had with my future bride didn't go so well. I offended her right off the bat with a lame question. Can you believe that, after class one day, I followed her to the cafeteria (not officially stalking . . .), I'd never spoken a word to her, and the first sentence out of my mouth as we stood in the lunch line was, "Do you mind if I ask you a personal question?" What did I just say? A "personal question?" That's smooth. What a way to introduce myself. Pathetic.

My opening line didn't totally turn her off . . . at least she let me ask my "personal question." I simply wanted to know why she was taking Greek. I'd never known a female who studied the original language of the New Testament. We had about thirty-five wannabe preachers in our class and two females, one of whom wore Army fatigues every day (and that definitely would not be Kim).

> THE FIRST CONVERSATION I HAD WITH MY FUTURE BRIDE DIDN'T GO SO WELL.

I knew immediately that I'd hit a land mine with that question. She looked at me like I was some kind of male chauvinist, a dragging-the-wife-by-the-hair caveman. And she didn't bat an eye as she responded that she was studying the language to prepare herself as a pastor. She pretty much shut me down.

By the time we'd made our way through the cafeteria line to check out, she turned to me and let me know that, actually, she wasn't really planning to be a pastor, she just wanted to learn the language for her own personal growth in Bible study. And with an air of finality and superiority, she tossed her head, picked up her tray, and walked away in defiance. Another man down. We can be so pathetic when it comes to verbally sparring with women, you know?

The confidence that led me to pursue her evaporated pretty quickly in the first five minutes of interacting with her. But I didn't give up. From the beginning, it was evident to me that she was one fierce woman. And I liked that. Kim's fierceness both attracted and intimidated me.

Kim's spirited response in that first conversation fueled my interest in her "like being drawn by the beauty and danger of climbing Mount Everest—the climb is filled with breathless anticipation and excitement, but woe to the man who attempts that climb unprepared!"[3]

Growing up in the foothills of the Ozarks, hunting was a way of life. Don't mean to offend, but we used guns. Double-barreled 12-gauge shotguns, single shot .22 caliber rifles, lever action 30-30s, and my personal favorite, Dad's M-1 carbine. We raised our own meat: chickens, hogs, and cows. What we didn't raise on our "rock farm," we shot—venison and squirrel. Combined with homegrown meat was the large supply of homegrown vegetables from the garden. There is nothing quite as good on a Sunday after church as "fresh fried chicken" (chicken that was walking around that morning).

When I met my wife, she'd never shot a gun or even been exposed to guns. Kimberly was a city girl—a genuine "Southern belle debutante." Her dad was a white-collar professional. The only hunting trip her family took was for a Christmas tree each year . . .

no firearm required there! She knew absolutely nothing about guns and had no interest in learning.

But right after we married, I decided to train my bride in the safe and proper use of a firearm. On a trip to my parents' home, I took her outside by the chicken house, walked off twenty-five paces, and put an empty can of evaporated milk at the base of an old locust tree. You could still see a fading picture of Elsie the cow on the label. I spent time showing Kim the basics of gun safety and carefully explained how to actually shoot the weapon.

When Kim raised the .25 caliber pistol to fire for the first time, she quickly lowered it and said, "I can't do this." I smiled and told her, "Sure you can, you can do this!" She raised the pistol again, this time with more determination. She took a breath and gently squeezed the trigger. The bullet left the chamber with a loud POP— bouncing the can and making dust fly. I thought to myself, "At least she was close," and went to see if I could tell where the bullet struck dirt. I picked up the can and was shocked to see a hole right through Elsie's nose!

YOUR WIFE MAY SEEM SUPERIOR TO YOU, BUT THE REALITY IS—SHE STILL NEEDS YOU.

Kim's shot couldn't have been more accurate. I said, "Lesson's over, great shot, we're done here." She seemed unimpressed and unaware of her natural skill. It would have taken me three or four shots to hit that can, and she nailed Elsie's nose her first try at firing a weapon.

As Kim's husband, I wanted to be her protector, defender, and rescuer, but once again, she unknowingly proved her superiority. She was a better marksman than I was and seemed to possess more skill at everything we attempted to do together. Can you relate?

Your wife may seem superior to you, but the reality is—she still needs you. She needs you to protect and lead her. She needs to be led by a man who is led by the Savior. That's God's design.

Why is fierceness in women so appealing to us? Let's admit it, we like the challenge. We admire the strength, courage, loyalty, and determination of a fierce woman. We like their spunk and passion. Fierce women don't grovel for attention and aren't desperate for a man to meet their deepest needs. I admire a woman who doesn't depend solely on a man for her identity or happiness.

But there are significant challenges that come with fulfilling the leadership role in the life of a fierce woman. Believe me, I know. I learned early on that I was no match for my fierce woman. She could outdebate me, outwit me, outshoot me, and definitely outdo me in levels of intensity.

Courage: It's Your Spiritual DNA

Adam was the first man to attempt to lead a fierce woman. God put him in a position that would require courage. Adam was given the opportunity to take a stand to obey God's command. As men, God places each of us in situations where we have the opportunity to reflect His ways and His character through exerting leadership. But leadership requires courage. And somehow it seems that a strong woman can be so intimidating that it sucks all desire from our hearts to lead. I felt like I could face the fiercest battle with men, but would run from the thought of facing a battle with my fierce wife.

But God created us to lead. He assigned us to lead. He's given us the mission to lead. That is at the core of what it means to be a man.

As we look at the first Adam—man of dust—do you sense a faint recollection like a dream, of what you were created to be? What you should be, what you desire to be? This is your DNA to live out courageous leadership, true manhood. When you read of men doing the extraordinary, of soldiers who give their lives in battle, when you watch the bravery of a hero, do you sense that stirring? Most of our lives, it lies buried beneath the drudgery and tedium of life, but when we hear of a true man who steps out courageously to face impossible odds . . . that stirring within is the remaining residue of the innate knowledge of what we were created to be before the fall. Our Creator's purpose for us rises within and reminds us of our mandate and our true identity.

We are the earthly reflection of Jesus: man of dust—man of heaven.

CHARACTERISTICS OF THE COURAGEOUS LEADER:

1. In strength and dignity he bears the image of God and his deepest identity is found in his relationship with Christ.
2. He fears God alone. His love for God is the motive that allows him to lead well.
3. He knows his assignment and lives to accomplish it.
4. When faced with overwhelming obstacles, and daunting challenges, he pushes past the pain and trusts in His God.
5. He accepts the mantle of leadership that God has placed upon him, seeing it not as a burden, but a privilege.
6. He knows that his strength lies solely in his humility before God and his complete dependence on Christ.
7. He is not ashamed to love with passion, conviction, and sacrifice.
8. If required, he willingly lays down his life for his God, God's truth, his wife, his children, or anyone else who should need a defender or rescuer.
9. He is generous with all he has, regretting only that he does not have more to give.
10. While others may wither, complain, or retreat in the storms of battle, trial, and affliction—by God's grace he is the warrior that continues to stand.
11. He is known as a man of his word.

12. He is known by his strength of character, and his tenderness of heart.

13. He wears the mantle of a prophet with conviction and courage but with a heart to administer grace to the listener.

14. As a recipient of God's grace and forgiveness, he freely extends God's grace and forgiveness to others.

15. His singular purpose is to glorify God.

Man, the earthly reflection of Jesus: man of dust—man of heaven.

You, me, we are both created to bear God's image. We can easily forget that. We can feel more like the "man of dust" (aka just a dirtbag), instead of realizing our significance as "men of heaven."

God knew we'd need that reminder and He included this encouraging word for us men of dust:

> Thus it is written, "The first man Adam became a living being"; the last Adam became a life-giving spirit. But it is not the spiritual that is first but the natural, and then the spiritual. The first man was from the earth, a man of dust; the second man is from heaven. As was the man of dust, so also are those who are of the dust, and as is the man of heaven, so also are those who are of heaven. Just as we have borne the image of the man of dust, we shall also bear the image of the man of heaven. (1 Corinthians 15:45–49)

As "sons of Adam" we struggle under the fallen conditions that plague us daily, but when we come to new life through the second Adam, we bear the image of the "man of heaven" and we operate from a position of victory. The battle is fierce, but the victory is already secure:

"But thanks be to God, who gives us the victory through our Lord Jesus Christ. Therefore, my beloved brothers, be steadfast, immovable, always abounding in the work of the Lord, knowing that in the Lord your labor is not in vain" (1 Corinthians 15:57–58).

As we struggle to live out our purpose as men, and typically fail in our attempts to be courageous leaders, we can lose sight of the "victory." I know that I have. Early in our marriage, my courage was tested and I failed repeatedly. I wanted to live that courageous life, I wanted to be the man of God that my wife needed, I wanted to be that tender warrior that could protect her from every danger, but leading a group of soldiers onto a real battlefield would've been less intimidating to me than actually leading my wife. In so many ways I felt like I was a disappointment.

The Man of Every Woman's Dreams

When I think of a real man, the epitome of manhood, the image of a Navy SEAL comes to mind. The Navy SEALs are one of the most elite Special Operations units in the world. Their motto: "Ready to Lead, Ready to Follow, Never Quit" inspires me to press on. I'm called to follow my God as I lead those entrusted to my care, and never quit—no matter how hard the assignment. These noble warriors stir my sense of duty. They live out the definition of a true hero: one who goes into harm's way for the benefit of another.

One of these heroes, Michael Monsoor, gave the ultimate gift of sacrifice as he laid down his life to protect his teammates. On September 29, 2006, Monsoor demonstrated exceptional bravery while standing guard on a rooftop in an insurgent-held sector of Ar Ramadi, Iraq. While under enemy fire, Petty Officer Monsoor took a position on the outcropping of the roof that protected his teammates, but exposed him to an insurgent's lob of a grenade. The grenade came from an unseen location, bounced off Monsoor's chest, and landed in front of him.

What is important to note in this heroic account is that Monsoor was in the position to take flight. He was the only SEAL on the roof that day who had an avenue of escape, and yet he chose to save his comrades. He was intentional and selfless, showing no regard for his own life, as he threw himself on the grenade, absorbing the blast with his own body.

MANHOOD AT ITS BEST SACRIFICES IN ORDER TO PROTECT OTHERS.

In 2008, President George W. Bush posthumously awarded Monsoor's parents their son's Medal of Honor. In the written citation from the president, Monsoor's sacrificial service was described and the closing comment states: "By his undaunted courage, fighting spirit, and unwavering devotion to duty in the face of certain death, Petty Officer Monsoor gallantly gave his life for country, thereby reflecting the highest traditions of the United States Naval Service."[4]

Monsoor's sacrifice was manhood on display. Manhood at its best sacrifices in order to protect others. Man of dust and man of heaven meet at the point of ultimate sacrifice. Every heroic sacrifice is an echo of that ultimate sacrifice as seen at the cross.

Jesus Christ is the true man that demonstrates the heart and soul, the core essence, of manhood. He is the One who laid down His life to secure our eternity. As the man of dust, He took on flesh to come as the warrior servant who would rescue His own. As the man of heaven, He will one day return as the warrior king to rescue His bride, the Church. He is the Man of every woman's dreams. He is the Man every man is created to image, to reflect. He is the example we're called to follow as real men.

But honestly, for many years I failed. I gave up. I lost hope. And I lost the courage to pick up that mantle of manhood. This book tells the story of how God rescued me, as a man, and how He rescued our marriage.

This warrior Savior invites you to follow Him into the battle. He is your faithful comrade, and He will not desert you or let you down.

It isn't too late. Will you join me as we pick up that mantle of manhood and courageously position ourselves to lead and protect those we love? As we walk through these pages together, I'll share with you more of our story, we'll look honestly at the common relationship dynamic between strong women and men like you and me, and I'll give you some practical help that has made a real difference in my life and in our marriage.

How about it? Are you up for the challenge?

Are you man enough to join me?

⚞ DIGGING IN ⚟

At the end of each chapter, we're going to dig into Scripture and I'll challenge you with a few diagnostic questions. We're calling this section "Digging In" because we're going to apply ourselves to a hard task—uncovering heart issues and mining out truths from Scripture that will provide weapons for our warfare. Make no mistake, you may feel like you're in a never-ending conflict with your wife, but we're not in a battle with flesh and blood. Your wife is not your enemy: ultimately, your battle is with the enemy of your soul, your own flesh, and the anti-God world system that surrounds us.

Jesus is our pattern for manhood and our model as a husband (Ephesians 5:23–32). In each section, we'll use His example from Scripture to help us dig in and discover what He has for us.

1. Today, begin this time by reading through John 1.

2. In our first chapter, we saw Jesus presented as the man of dust and man of heaven (1 Corinthians 15:45–49). We see Him literally become that when He takes on flesh (John 1:14). Spend some time thanking Him for being willing to step into history and come as your Rescuer.

3. Jesus' first public action was to begin His ministry by submitting to baptism, not because He was sinful, but because this was a public "sign" of His commission by the Father (John 1:29–34). After this, He began inviting men to "follow Him." Are you willing to "follow Him" as we take this journey together? What kind of sacrifices did men make to follow Jesus? What kind will you make?

4. Your purpose, as a man, is to reflect this Man, and that is a significant calling. As you read through the list of "Characteristics of the Courageous Leader" (pp. 25–26), which ones encouraged you? Choose three today that you believe are most needed in your life right now and ask God to begin supplying the grace and power to walk in obedience to Him by intentionally applying God's Word to those areas.

5. Before going on to the next chapter, spend some time asking God to provide you with His help as you work through the material in this book. Make prayer a priority as we take this journey together (1 John 5:14–15, 20).

The Passive Deserter

❦

The only place outside Heaven where you can be perfectly safe
from all the dangers and perturbations of love is Hell.[1]

C. S. Lewis

Clint Miller[2] had the rugged good looks and build to catch any woman's eye. He carried himself with confidence and commandeered the respect of the men under his leadership at his company. Clint was intelligent, witty, respected by friends, and admired by his competitors. He had only attended our church sporadically for about six months, but he seemed knowledgeable about Scripture and openly shared his conversion testimony and commitment to Christ. Clint was what many might call a real "man's man." His children showed visible respect and fondness for their dad. He appeared to be courageous and a man of integrity. He was diligent, industrious, interesting, humorous, strong, frank, and conservative in his values and convictions.

Clint Miller was a likeable man and . . . Clint Miller was a deserter.

Talking in the parking lot of the softball field, both of us stood with one foot resting on the tailgate of his pickup truck. As the conversation grew serious, I thought I was listening to a man confiding his need for marital counsel. He was listing many of the same complaints I'd had in the past about my own marriage. He told me about how his wife was making his life miserable, how she questioned his every decision, how she nagged at him and made him feel more like a child than a man. But then he went an entirely different direction than what I expected.

Clint went down the road of justifying a decision to leave his wife and children. He built his case on the premise that God's will for our lives is our personal happiness. He was thoroughly convinced that God would bless his decision to find happiness by "starting over" with someone else and stressed that he'd figured out it wasn't really God's will for him to marry his wife in the first place;

WHEN YOU ARE AIDING AND ABETTING THE ENEMY OF YOUR OWN SOUL, YOU WILL EVENTUALLY BECOME ITS CAPTIVE.

that he wasn't right with God at the time, so by leaving her he could rectify that. His thinking had strayed so far from the truth of God's Word that he really believed God would be pleased as he deserted his wife and children.

In the weeks that followed, no amount of coercion by me, or others, was able to convince him otherwise. Soon after he left his wife and children, he left our church as well and joined a church that condoned his actions.

The Deserter's Profile

A deserter is one who fails to keep his commitment. He runs from duty. He breaks his promise of fidelity. He leaves his post. He gives up.

The picture of Bowe Bergdahl pops in my head when I think of a deserter. This young man walked away from his post, his unit, his commitment, and his nation. While all of the details have not been disclosed (and may never be), this much we know: the enemy eventually took him hostage.

Most of us have experienced some type of desertion or at least read of dramatic ones that impact wars and revolutions. But the ironic thing about being a deserter is how deserting eventually becomes your downfall.

The spiritual lesson is this: when you are aiding and abetting the enemy of your own soul, you will eventually become its captive.

When it comes to desertion, one particular name comes to mind every time: Demas. Demas was a defector and a deserter. When he first comes on the scene, we see him fighting for the faith alongside the Apostle Paul and other faithful fellow laborers in ministry. Demas was, for a time, "a good soldier of Christ Jesus" (2 Timothy 2:3). But at some point, Demas began to grow weary of the fight (2 Timothy 4:7). He grew tired of being tired. He began to entertain thoughts of leaving his friends, leaving the aged apostle, and departing from "the faith that was once for all delivered to the saints" (Jude 3).

Apparently Demas was with Paul during his imprisonment in Rome. But at some point, Demas deserted his friend and mentor. Although we don't have all the details, one thing that we do know is, one day Demas left. He walked away. By his actions he said: "This is not worth it. Forget it. I'm out of here."

I've heard that "fatigue makes cowards of us all," and maybe that was part of it. We've all been there. At our lowest point, we've all indulged in deserter-fantasies: "Just leave, take off, I deserve better than this! I'm done. I don't have to put up with this anymore!"

As Paul writes Timothy, he mentions the desertion:

"Do your best to come to me soon. For Demas, in love with this present world, has deserted me and gone to Thessalonica . . ." (2 Timothy 4:9–10).

Paul describes Demas's heart as "in love with this present world."

His heart was the problem. We aren't sure of the details, but his heart turned and set its affection on something else. He deserted his first love (Christ) and "followed his heart" that fell in love with "this present world." That could mean anything from being in love with comfort and ease to being in love with sensual and immoral pleasure.

Demas was probably not that different from you and me. He probably reached the point where he decided he didn't want to do the hard thing anymore. It was just too tough to keep on.

Heading to My Cave

I've been there. I never abandoned my family physically, but I did emotionally. When life required too much from me, I escaped. I took off. I headed to my cave. I wasn't thinking about how it affected anyone else, I was in survival mode.

When it came to functioning with my wife, heading to the cave was my default position. Ever done that? How's that working out for you? Actually, it wasn't too helpful for our relationship. I've asked Kim to jump in here to say a few words about how my passivity affected her. If you tend to run from conflict or shut down emotionally, it might be affecting your wife in a similar way.

(Kim): When LeRoy would run to his cave, it only made things worse. For years we were caught in the grip of the same destructive cycle that plagued the first couple and has been repeated for thousands of years since. It's what we call the Fierce Woman/Fearful Man cycle. In this cycle, a strong woman (usually unintentionally) intimidates her husband or frustrates him with her intensity. He retreats, so she increases the pressure, hoping he'll respond to her need. The cycle might work something like this:

Wife has strong desires and "exerts her fierceness" in order to obtain those desires . . .

Husband retreats in fear . . . OR

Husband ignores wife and picks up the nearest brain-numbing object available (media remote, newspaper, laptop) . . . OR

Husband fears disappointing wife and goes to any length to make sure she gets what she wants . . . OR

Husband feels intimidated and lashes back in anger resulting in verbal or physical injury.[3]

Do you see yourself in this cycle? I remember just wanting LeRoy to engage with me in communication. I could pour out my heart to him on something I thought was extremely important, and he'd never look me in the eye. He'd drop his head and look at the floor. His lack of response was extremely frustrating and so disappointing to me that I would lash out in anger, or have an emotional meltdown.

> **THE FURTHER HE RETREATED, THE MORE MY FIERCENESS GREW.**

LeRoy's passivity was repulsive to me, so I fought back the only way I knew how. I would demean him verbally or I would appeal to him through tears. I kept thinking he would respond in strength, that he would take the lead and provide me with a sense of security and hope, but instead of leading me, he just went further into his cave.

The further he retreated, the more my fierceness grew. In one of the few sessions we had with a marital counselor, the counselor asked me to answer what I would want most—if I could have anything at all from LeRoy. My answer was: "More than anything else, I just want him to pray with me." The male counselor seemed stunned and incredulous. "Really, that's what you'd want most from him?" Yes, that's what women need most, whether they realize it or not.

Within all women, we desire for our husband to step up to the plate and lead us. We crave his spiritual leadership! I believe God placed that need within us. No matter how strong your wife is she needs to know that you are going to live out your purpose as a man of God—no matter what. If she knows that is your determination, and you are demonstrating that you're committed to her and you're committed to God—your wife will follow you.

(LeRoy): Okay, I just wanted you to hear a bit from my fierce woman, because it's helpful to learn how our wives feel when we desert our post. Kim will share the fierce woman's perspective from time to time as we work our way through this journey.

When Kim and I lead marriage retreats, I challenge the men to make the commitment to pray with their wives nightly. Recently we returned to a church where I issued that challenge a few years previously. A middle-aged couple I recognized from when I'd been at the church the first time approached me. The wife asked her husband if he wanted to tell me what had happened to them since that marriage retreat. She was tearful as he confided to me that he took that challenge to begin praying with her, but he hadn't expected it to be that hard. He couldn't understand why it would be so difficult to do such a simple thing, but he kept at it, even though it was humbling. He told me that, although it was extremely hard in the beginning, he kept that commitment and had prayed with his wife every night for the past three years since accepting that challenge. Taking that responsibility seriously made a profound impact on their relationship.

As I watched the wife's reaction to what he was telling me, it was obvious that his spiritual leadership had affected her dramatically. Perhaps the most important aspect of this conversation was the fact that their adult daughter and son-in-law were listening to what he was saying. As I turned and noticed them standing there, holding a newborn, I challenged the son-in-law to take seriously his spiritual leadership role and follow the example that his father-in-law had set for him in praying daily with his wife.

Maybe you're reading this and your wife doesn't know God or

care anything about spiritual matters—she still needs you to be the man of God. Even if your wife doesn't realize it, she needs to be led spiritually—that is her heart's deepest need. Demonstrating spiritual leadership provides the security that your wife craves.

If you emotionally check out, you can't lead your wife.

If you've withdrawn to a cave, your wife is probably trying to pull you out of that cave. She may yell, cry, bribe, threaten, or demean you, in an attempt to wake you up to the desperate nature of the situation and call you back to your post! Passivity is repulsive to women. No matter how strong your woman is, no matter how much she may grab the reins of leadership, the truth is—women want their men to lead.

I want you to know, even though my wife is very strong, even "fierce," and we were in the grips of the destructive "Fierce Woman/ Fearful Man" cycle for years . . . we now enjoy a unified complementary relationship where mutual respect, tenderness, compassion, humility, and lovingkindness are the norm. We are both quick to admit when we've wronged the other and quick to offer (or ask for) forgiveness. Those components are huge in developing a relationship that is beneficial and enjoyable—and most importantly one that glorifies God. (I'll be sharing some practical ways those components can be developed in chapters 6–10.)

WHAT FIERCE WOMEN REALLY NEED

We saw in chapter 1 that we were created to be courageous leaders, but like Adam, we're prone to passivity. When I started off in our marriage, I was confident that I'd make a great husband. In fact, I was foolish enough to think that any woman would feel privileged to have me. (How's that for getting real?) I had a lot to learn about women. But one of the most important things we men need to learn is how to lead a strong woman rather than run from her.

Most of us feel utterly incapable of leading our wife spiritually. And innately, we know that this constitutes our greatest failure. Knowing we fail as spiritual leaders becomes the echo of Adamic failure ringing incessantly in our weary soul. We know what we ought to do, who we're to be, but we're constantly confronted with crippling incompetence. We're driven to retreat in morbid silence, licking our wounds. We play the victim, rather than playing the man. We hate ourselves for it, hate our life. And bitterness settles in. Bitterness toward our wife, and bitterness toward the Lord. In bitterness we retreat. We desert our post. It's just too much.

We want to be that courageous leader that we talked about in the last chapter, but it seems an impossible role to step into. That guy has it all together, not me. If you're like most of us "nice guys," you probably relate more to the characteristics of a passive deserter than the hero we saw in the last chapter.

CHARACTERISTICS OF THE PASSIVE DESERTER:

1. His identity is shaped by his failures and weaknesses.

2. Fear drives most of his decisions and actions. Often he is a people pleaser and wants to be well liked. He lives from the motive of getting love rather than living from the motive of loving God and others.

3. Passivity is his default position. He is too crippled by fear, insecurity, and the belief that he can't do anything right to attempt to tackle any leadership responsibility.

4. Past failures often prevent him from persevering when faced with challenges and obstacles.

5. The guilt of deserting his leadership post becomes an oppressive burden and pressure that saps him of strength, confidence, and hope.

6. He operates in weakness because he is depending on his own strength, independent from God.

7. He is too defeated to live or love passionately.

8. He reacts to painful circumstances and conflict by running or hiding in order to protect himself.

9. He hoards what he has, living in the mode of self-protection.

10. He is no warrior; he withers, complains, or retreats in the storms of battle.

11. He tends to exaggerate, excuse, self-justify, and will even lie if necessary, in order to protect himself from painful consequences. You cannot depend on what he says.

12. Sarcasm, insulting statements, and rude behavior are used to mask his spiritual weakness. His self-focus prevents compassion or tenderness.

13. He is too insecure to speak truth in love. His self-absorption with his own "perceived injuries" prevents him from being able to come alongside others who are in need of healing and grace.

14. He relishes the role of victim; he believes he is "owed an apology" and therefore is unable to extend grace and forgiveness. He is unaware or unappreciative of God's grace that has been demonstrated to him.

15. His singular purpose is to protect himself.

Desertion comes in many forms. Physically, emotionally, spiritually, and sexually, men are deserting their wives. While we were working on this chapter, thousands of marriages were rocked by the revelation of the Ashley Madison hacking. By the time you read these words, the Ashley Madison scandal will be old news, but the wake of destruction left by its clientele will still be churning.

Ashley Madison was established in 2001 for the purpose of arranging "adulterous opportunities." It was launched as an "online adultery business" in 2010 by Noel Biderman, who declares: "Monogamy, in my opinion is a failed experiment."[4] The website's trademark byline reads: "Life is short, have an affair." We haven't seen it, but according to news reports, the website's home page features a woman holding her finger to her lips as if to indicate "Keep quiet, don't tell." But Ashley Madison wasn't able to keep its client's personal affair history quiet. The hack revealed over 37 million names and the account information of those individuals who signed up with the intention to seek out a sexual affair. The number is staggering. But it is also revealing.

We live in a nation of adultery. Men and women are seeking happiness and fulfillment through illicit encounters and immoral sexual activity. Marriage vows lack the binding commitment they represent. Men, by the millions, are deserting their posts, flippantly tossing aside their fidelity, and leaving their wives and families to deal with the devastation caused by their selfishness.

In contrast, some men don't react in passivity, or seek out adulterous sexual exploits, but when they are confronted by their wife's fierceness they respond in a show of force. It becomes a battle. A battle of the sexes. Who can outdebate the other? Who can match blow for blow until one gives up? Who can demonstrate superior intellect?

Round after round, they trade railing for railing, hit for hit, never minding the damage to the emotions or the psyche of the wife or the collateral damage to the children. Some men don't stop at verbal punches, but actually lash out physically. Note: There is never, I repeat, NEVER a justification for resorting to a physically or sexually abusive response to a deeply spiritual problem. These extremes may not be true of you, but you may still be living as a deserter. You may be so far gone that you believe there is no hope, but trust me, there is. There is an answer to your marital crisis!

Your Mission Impossible

The answer is not to withdraw or to retreat. The answer won't be found through seeking another woman's affections or by building entrenchments and fighting it out. God's ways and wisdom are far above every husband's way of dealing with this issue. The reason why this seems so hard is because . . . get ready for this . . . it seems so hard because *it is hard!* It is not only hard—it is impossible. (Encouraging news, I know, but hang on, I'm not finished.)

Do you remember how Jesus' disciples responded to the question about divorce? Jesus made it clear that God's plan from the beginning was a monogamous and committed relationship for life. The disciples seemed shocked by Jesus' sobering description and serious approach to marriage. They were so taken aback by what He said that they determined it might be best to avoid marriage altogether:

"The disciples said to him, 'If such is the case of a man with his wife, it is better not to marry'" (Matthew 19:10).

It sounds like they thought marital fidelity and a commitment to courageous leadership in marriage is impossible! News flash: It is impossible—if we're attempting it in our own strength.

Do you really believe that you can do all things through Christ who strengthens you? Do you believe that with God all things are possible? That nothing is too hard for Him? Your weakness, my weakness, can actually serve us well—when it serves as a compass pointing us to True North. If our weakness drives us to search out truths from His sure eternal, perfect, living, undefeatable Word, then it serves us well. His Word provides the answer to how we navigate our "mission impossible." If our weakness leads us to place our dependence on the One who never deserts us, then our weakness serves us well.

As men, we must look to one Man who sets the example for us all when it comes to fidelity and courage. This Man is the ultimate example of the committed bridegroom. He provides the key to standing at your post when you're tempted to desert. Fastening our eyes on this perfect Man, laying down His bloody body on the cross as the atoning sacrifice—true love in action, provides us with the defining example of the faithful bridegroom.

As Christian men, we know our "impossible" assignment:

"Husbands, love your wives, just as Christ also loved the church and gave Himself up for her . . ." (Ephesians 5:25 NASB).

Just reading those words "love your wives, just as Christ . . . loved . . ." lays out a parallel of staggering proportions! Talk about mission impossible. How can we begin to "love as Christ loved"? Just that assignment alone is enough to tempt us to throw in the towel, to walk away, to desert our post.

But even though Jesus challenges us to an impossible assignment, He doesn't leave us without a battle strategy to tackle the mission impossible. God knew we'd grow weary and overwhelmed, that we'd lose heart and be tempted to give up. So He gave us a battle plan:

> . . . let us run with endurance the race that is set before us, fixing our eyes on Jesus, the author and perfecter of faith, who for the joy set before Him endured the cross, despising the shame . . . For consider Him who has endured such hostility by sinners against Himself, so that you will not grow weary and lose heart (Hebrews 12:1–3 NASB).

Looking to Christ as your example, depending on Him to provide strength and endurance for the assignment of loving your wife, for running the race that is set before you, is the key to accomplishing your mission impossible.

To fight this battle, you must stop fighting. Your strength to be what you cannot be on your own must be found in owning up to the fact that you have NO strength on your own. The strength to love your wife will not come from striving, but can only come from dependence on God's work in your life. The strength to tackle your mission impossible will come through quietness and confidence.

"For thus saith the Lord God, the Holy One of Israel . . . in quietness and in confidence shall be your strength . . ." (Isaiah 30:15 KJV).

In quietness and confidence shall be your strength:

In quietness (stop striving) and confidence (start trusting) shall be your strength. In quietness (not passivity, but actively resting in His work on the cross) and confidence (not arrogance or self-willed determination, but strength to stand because of humility before the Lord) will be your strength. In quietness (not the silent treatment or withdrawal) and confidence (security that comes from your relationship with Christ) will be your strength. In quietness (not winning through debate, but winning your wife's heart through your life's example) and confidence (a devotion to God that she will respect and follow) will be your strength.

> **TO LOVE YOUR WIFE, YOU MUST FIRST LOVE CHRIST DEEPLY.**

This will be your strength to stand at your post, to lead, to face the fiercest battles with courage.

A wife's refusal to follow her husband's leadership is not solely based on her strength of personality or the dynamics of her emotional makeup. Her refusal to follow more often results from her husband's weak, lackluster love for Christ. You may say, "I love the Lord, but I don't know how to love my wife." Your love for your wife (and all others) will flow from your deepening love for Christ. In order to truly love your wife, you need to direct your heart, mind, and affections toward Christ first. To love your wife, you must first love Christ deeply.

Love on Display

The young husband came into my office on a sunny afternoon with a dark storm raging in his soul. He nervously sat down in the chair in front of my desk to pour it all out, "Pastor, I was on my way to commit suicide." He'd failed his wife again. His immorality and sexual addiction seemed impossible to conquer. Suicide wasn't the answer to his deep shame. Suicide wasn't necessary to conquer his immoral desires. Cultivating a greater love for his Savior than the love for his sin was the only solution that finally brought him victory.

It may sound strange or foreign, as a man, to think about "cultivating love for Jesus," but there is nothing more manly than responding in love to the love that's been poured out on us. As I follow the admonition in Hebrews 12 to "fix my eyes on Jesus," to consider and focus on His merciful and redemptive work in rescuing me, it deepens my love for Him.

Love is not seen or experienced in a vacuum, but must be put on display through actual demonstration. Love isn't a theory or concept but an active process. The nature of love requires that it be shown—demonstrated through action. God demonstrated His love to us in the most horrific and painful event—bleeding to death on a cross. The cross is where God's love for sinners is most clearly seen. In the same way, He invites us to experience that work of love in our deepest moments of struggle. The work of the cross can enter into every painful aspect of our inability to be what we know we should be. Our sinful failure is the very place where God desires to demonstrate what His love looks like. That is love on display.

His love for you is clearly seen when His commitment to you stands firm in your darkest hour. Your love for Him is displayed as you remain faithful when everything in you urges you to leave. Love is demonstrated when we walk out of our cave of protection and pick up our mantle of leadership.

It's not easy, but whoever said manhood is about taking the easy way out?

Who's with me?

⊰ DIGGING IN ⊱

1. The steadfast, covenant love that God extends to us is our greatest assurance and comfort. He has promised to never leave or forsake us (Hebrews 13:5) and is unswerving in His commitment. Spend some moments thanking God for the security that His character provides.

2. No one has ever endured greater temptation to desert a mission than what Jesus faced in Matthew 4:1–11. Consider Jesus' reaction to Satan when he offered a "shortcut" to avoid the cross. How can you respond when you are faced with the temptation to desert your leadership post in your marriage?

3. Read through the "Characteristics of the Passive Deserter" on pages 38–39 and then consider whether you recognize yourself in any of these. If so, repent of ways you've deserted your wife as her spiritual leader, or ways you've been passive in your manhood. Ask Jesus to show you how you can reflect His characteristics of faithfulness to your wife. Ask her to forgive you for ways you've failed to do this.

Anything You Can Do, She Can Do Better!

$\longrightarrow \diamond \longleftarrow$

As far as I can tell, real men don't have a problem
with smart, successful women.

But they do mind being castrated. It's a guy thing.[1]

KATHLEEN PARKER, SYNDICATED COLUMNIST

Although she's different from my wife in most every way,
my mom could also be considered a "fierce woman." I'll
never forget the day I watched her stand her ground
against a beast that outweighed her by almost a ton. We were what
you might call "rock farmers." We lived on eighty acres of rock and
some patches of pasture where we kept a few chickens and cows. We
had one troublesome heifer who kept getting out of the pasture and
leading other cows out with her, and it was time to take this rebel to
the sale barn.

I was about fourteen years old and was attempting to help my
mom lead the heifer through a narrow loading chute into the old

'63 GMC pickup. My job was to insert a 2x4 in between the slats of the chute as my mom coaxed the heifer from behind. While my mom yelled and clapped to pressure the heifer forward, I slipped the board behind the cow, at each section of the chute, to prevent her from reversing course and bolting out of the chute. We'd made a little progress up the chute, and as I pulled out the board to reset it, the heifer spun around in a space that looked impossible to do a 180—but she did! As she wheeled around, she struck my five-foot-two, ninety-seven-pound mom full force to the head.

Mom was knocked back several feet inside the corral, landing in the muck of mud and cow manure—the consistency of wet concrete. Covered with wet black muck, manure, and mud, blood poured from her forehead, and I thought she was dead. Before I could jump the fence to get to her, Mom scrambled to her feet, grabbed a board, and began whacking that wide-eyed beast so furiously that the terrified heifer went straight up the loading chute into the bed of our truck! I was stunned. That day, I gained a new respect for Mom, and it gave me a small glimpse into the strength of a woman.

From that day, I knew that a strong woman was not to be messed with. I admired strong women, but I never realized that I could be intimidated by that strength, that is, until I met my wife. Facing my fears came easier when it involved pushing my body to its limits, like when I dove into the river or ran the bleachers fifty times, but as I grew into manhood, I learned that facing fears related to women was a completely different ballgame. Nothing compares to the kind of glorious exhilaration or debilitating fear that a fierce woman can evoke.

(Kim): Proving that I could "outdo my man" was never my plan. I never intended to compete with, or conquer my husband, but in the "Fierce Woman/Fearful Man" relationship, that is what the man feels his wife is doing. And it often begins as a result of the differences you bring into a marriage.

LeRoy and I are different. What an understatement. Early in our marriage, our differences erupted in painful conflicts regularly, well to be honest, pretty much daily. Rather than appreciating and growing from the expression of those differences, the differences became a means of evaluation and competition. A standard of superior versus inferior began to emerge. (Remember his story of teaching me to shoot a gun?) And, although "my way" of doing things wasn't truly superior, I gave every indication that it was.

J. I. Packer gives a comical illustration of this in *Weakness Is the Way*:

> A *Peanuts* cartoon from way back when has Lucy asking a glum-looking Charlie Brown what he is worrying about. Says Charlie, "I feel inferior." "Oh," says Lucy, "you shouldn't worry about that. Lots of people have that feeling." "What, that they're inferior?" Charlie asks. "No," Lucy replies, "that you're inferior."

Commenting on that exchange, Packer states, "It illustrates . . . how easily those who, rightly or wrongly, think themselves strong can rub in and make fester the sense of weakness that others already have."[2]

Does your wife ever treat you in a way that leaves you feeling "emasculated"? Does it feel like you can never do anything right? Like she's far superior to you?

That's how LeRoy felt, but that isn't at all what I intended to do to him. Our family backgrounds were completely different. My family welcomed debate and practiced it loudly and with frequency. His father ruled with an iron fist and no one spoke a word to disagree. LeRoy grew up in a blue-collar family, in a rural area, and had daily chores like milking cows and gathering eggs from chickens (or would it be hens?). His family never traveled, ate out, or shopped in malls. My father was a mechanical engineer and started a small business that provided a comfortable living for our family (I might've been a little spoiled).

I feel at home in large cities and upscale social environments. LeRoy doesn't. At all. In high school, I was one of a small group of young women invited to be a member of an exclusive (and fairly snobbish) social convention that has been practiced in the South for generations (ever heard of a debutante?). During the season of my life where I was being "introduced to society" and entertained in wealthy homes with lavish meals, LeRoy was working a full-time job to save money for college, and fixing fences to keep cows in the pasture.

When I was in college, my family took a trip to Hawaii and I brought LeRoy back a T-shirt. He said that's probably the closest he would ever get to reaching the "Big Island."

Besides the difference in family backgrounds, there is the difference in our personalities. He's an introvert, I'm an extrovert. He depends on God's grace to function in large crowds; I say, "The more the merrier!" He is wired with the need for solitude and a slower pace. Me, not so much.

While working on this book, we had the opportunity to revisit one of the original sources of painful conflict in our marriage, that is, big-city life, coupled with the pressure of meetings, large crowds, and a packed schedule. And I couldn't help but wonder if God allowed that "revisit" to remind us of how dark our days once were, and to see how far He's brought us.

We'd only been married a year when we moved from the rural countryside to downtown Dallas. The transition was difficult for LeRoy, and I viewed his personal distress as weakness. I was too immature to recognize and appreciate his differences, and in my pride, I demeaned him for those differences. Five years into our marriage, I realized that the confident, happy, driven young man I'd married was gone. In his place was a withdrawn, fearful, insecure, and miserable man who believed he could never measure up to my expectations. And in a moment of honesty, LeRoy confessed (after I pressed for an answer), that he no longer loved me.

Maybe you're there now. Hopeless. Maybe you believe that things will never improve, that you'll never be free to lead your wife because she dismisses you as "inferior" or treats you with disdain. If you feel emasculated or unappreciated by your wife or by women in general, you aren't alone in feeling invalidated as a man. If you're married to a fierce woman, not only do you have her fierceness to contend with, the entire culture seems intent on stripping men of their man-card.

Where Have All the Men Gone?

As our society has demonized traditional structures and blurred clear role distinctions, young men are insecure and confused about what masculinity looks like and how they should function as a male. There is gender confusion, but also a lack of understanding of the responsibilities and challenges of manhood. Albert Mohler, president of The Southern Baptist Theological Seminary, addressed this problem more than a decade ago:

> We now face the phenomenon of perpetual boyhood on the part of many males. Refusing to grow up, these young men function as boys well into their twenties—some even into their thirties and beyond. An extended male adolescence marks the lifestyles, expectations, and behavior of far too many young males, whose masculine identity is embraced awkwardly, if at all.[3]

In 2008 a survey of 2,000 men and women provided a telling picture of the perception of what it means to "be a man" in the twenty-first century. More than half the men stated that they felt society is turning them into "waxed and coiffed metrosexuals" and 52 percent said they had to live according to women's rules.[4]

As we work on this manuscript, we're witnessing the world's adulation of a "man" that some are praising for the "heroic courage" to undergo the surgical transformation to become a "woman." He even received a prestigious "Woman of the Year" award. We're experiencing a seismic societal upheaval when it comes to gender distinctions. Men have never looked more confused and seemingly unsure of what it means to "be a man."

Could it be that women bear some of the responsibility for the loss of manliness?

One friend told me that the theme song in her marriage could be titled: "Anything you can do, I can do better!" She then went on to describe how that attitude had damaged their relationship. This is a woman who loves Jesus, loves His Word, and claims to love her husband—but for years she treated him as inferior, as "less." She didn't begin marriage with the plan to destroy her husband, but that's what she did.

In *Fierce Women*, I share an acronym using the word EMASCULATION to spell out how we women can unintentionally strip our husbands of their manhood (in a sense). I simply put down on paper a graphically honest description of myself (combined with a few other women I've known) and the profile of a destructively fierce woman began to emerge.

EMASCULATION:

Ego-deflating treatment:
  * Criticism that demeans
  * Comparison
  * Questioning his decisions regularly
  * Mothering/Smothering
  * Dream destroying

Manipulation
- ❋ Behavior modification (similar to puppy training techniques)
- ❋ Exerting pressure (to get my way or get him to take care of responsibilities)
- ❋ Hidden agenda behind syrupy sweetness and batting eyelashes
- ❋ Withholding sex or using it for bribery

Aggression
- ❋ Taking forceful action to get what you want
- ❋ Pushy attitude, tone, and words
- ❋ Hit-n-Run tactics (setting up an emotional minefield for him to weave his way through)

Selfishness
- ❋ Self-focused/self-absorbed
- ❋ Self-serving
- ❋ Prone to self-pity

Controlling
- ❋ Dominating
- ❋ Fearful of outcome if not calling the shots
- ❋ Attempting to change husband

Unrestrained words
- ❋ Too much talking!!!
- ❋ Tone plus facial expression/body language which communicates he's an idiot, worthless, or can never do anything right
- ❋ Using words as weapons

Leaving your husband hungry for attention
- ❋ Ignoring his needs
- ❋ Not making him a priority
- ❋ Letting yourself go

"Anything you can do, I can do better"
* Competitive rather than supportive
* Superior attitude
* Intimidating

Taking charge
* Impatient, unwilling to wait for husband to act
* Taking over his areas of responsibility
* Saying he's the leader while you make all the decisions

Independent living
* Pursuing separate interests
* Living in your own world (romance novels, Facebook, Internet, friends, church)
* Keeping secrets from him

Obnoxiously opinionated
* Convinced yours is the only way
* Treating preference issues as absolutes
* Unteachable and unwilling to listen

No margins
* Spending time with your man is squeezed out by your over-filled schedule
* He's not an important priority to you and he knows it
* No time to build an intimate emotional bond through date-nights or weekend excursions

I'm ashamed to admit it, but much of this list described me our first fifteen years. And you know what? I've had tons of women tell me that list describes them exactly. And it stunned them. They never even considered that their well-meaning "help" was completely deflating their husband's desire to lead. They never imagined that they were actually "emasculating" their man.

I want to offer you this thought: If you and your wife are struggling in a destructive relationship dynamic right now, she may not even realize how her well-intentioned behavior is affecting you. You may think she's your biggest enemy, while she keeps wondering what in the world is wrong with you.

The tendency to emasculate, demean, and deconstruct manhood seems to be in the woman's DNA. It comes far too easily to us. And what I want you to know is that your wife probably doesn't even realize that's what she's doing. In *Fierce Women*, I explain what I believe lies at the root of our desire to control men. Here's an excerpt of what I share with wives:

The Desire to Control

Eve's choice of the forbidden led to her curse, and every woman since Eve has had to contend with it. "To the woman he said, 'I will surely multiply your pain in childbearing; in pain you shall bring forth children. Your desire shall be for your husband, and he shall rule over you'" (Genesis 3:16).

When I was younger, I thought the phrase "Your desire shall be for your husband" referred to having some kind of insatiable desire for my husband either emotionally or physically. But when I dug a little deeper and checked out some reputable commentaries, I discovered this curse contains an interesting Hebrew word found only one other time in Scripture.

In Genesis 4:7 we find the other time the word translated "desire" is used, and it's in reference to sin wanting to dominate or overpower Cain:

> If you do well, will you not be accepted? And if you do not do well, sin is crouching at the door. Its desire is for you, but you must rule over it.

Notice that "sin" is crouching, ready to pounce, ready to "overcome" and subdue Cain. "Its *desire* is for you . . ." That word "desire" is the urge to dominate. Any honest woman will tell you she struggles with this. It's the urge to control. And it's ugly.

According to pastor John MacArthur:

> Because of sin and the curse, the man and the woman will face struggles in their own relationship. Sin has turned the harmonious system of God-ordained roles into distasteful struggles of self-will. Life-long companions, husbands and wives, will need God's help in getting along as a result. The woman's desire will be to lord it over her husband, but the husband will rule by divine design (Ephesians 5:22–25). This interpretation of the curse is based upon the identical Hebrew words and grammar being used in Genesis 4:7. . . to show the conflict man will have with sin as it seeks to rule him.[5]

The flip side of the woman's calling to be a helper is the curse of . . . controlling. We want to control our husbands. The good stuff God put in us, which makes us a beautifully fierce woman and an effective helper, gets perverted and twisted into this dangerous tool of domination that we use to "whip the man into shape."[6]

So, our DNA is to "control" our man . . . but at the same time, most men have a dangerous component at work that actually provides fuel for the woman's ability to emasculate him. That dangerous component has a name: passivity. A destructive cycle forms as the wife exerts her dominance, and the husband caves to his passive nature: The Fierce Woman/Fearful Man cycle. A couple can live in the black hole of this cycle their entire marriage.

LeRoy thought things would never improve. He'd given up hope. What he saw as his attempts to be a good guy, nice husband, noncombatant, was actually the dangerous component of passivity that held him captive and prevented him from stepping up to take the lead, to confront me in my sin and lead us out of our black hole. Listen to his perspective on how he confused being a "good Christian husband" with passivity.

The Quiet Man

(LeRoy): When we were in the middle of a heated verbal exchange, my natural inclination was to go quiet. I was fine with letting Kim "win." I knew arguing with her was a hopeless cause and I knew I had nothing to prove, so being quiet seemed like the "noble" course to take. In the last chapter I told you, "The strength to tackle your mission impossible will come through quietness and confidence." There is a time for quiet, but not when "quiet" is a means of self-protection rather than the action of leadership. In 2008, Sarah Womack wrote an article highlighting the results of research revealing that the modern man feels emasculated:

> Many men believe the world is now dominated by women and that they have lost their role in society, fuelling feelings of depression and being undervalued.
>
> Research shows the extent to which men have had to change within one or two generations, adapting to new rules and different expectations.
>
> Men said they "felt handcuffed" by political correctness—only 33 per cent felt they could speak freely and say what they thought, whereas two thirds found it safer to conceal their opinions.
>
> Harvey Mansfield, a Harvard professor and America's best-known political philosopher, who tackles the topic in his book *Manliness*, says the issue is ignored.
>
> "A man has to be embarrassed about being a man. I am trying to bring back the word manliness. It's not respected," he said.
>
> According to the survey, men hold other men who speak their

mind in high regard . . . Their biggest hero is Churchill.

But four out of ten are frightened of heights and spiders while a third are frightened of bossy women.[7]

Although we're seeing a seismic cultural shift in regard to gender issues, the fear of strong women isn't a new development. The first time we see a man drop the ball of leadership is in the first marriage, when the man stood quietly at his wife's side, while she faced temptation and the enemy's lies. Scripture records no attempts by Adam to take action or "dominion" over this creature. He just stood still and let the woman do the talking.

"So when the woman saw that the tree was good for food, and that it was a delight to the eyes, and that the tree was to be desired to make one wise, she took of its fruit and ate, and she also gave some to her husband who was *with her*, and he ate" (Genesis 3:6, emphasis mine).

Did you see that? The woman ate, and handed the forbidden fruit right over to her spiritual leader who abdicated his position of authority. While Eve conversed with the enemy, Adam stood silently and then followed her lead into spiritual death.

As men, we are working from the same template: Adam. He was the first image bearer, but also the first man to drop his sword and shield in failure. He transferred to all of us "sons of Adam," a somewhat confused spiritual heritage.

On one hand, we know that as sons of God we have a high and noble calling. On the other hand, we are painfully aware of our failure to live out that calling consistently. We desire to be the spiritual leader for our wife and little ones, but struggle with falling short in that area regularly.

Every male and female, in every generation of every culture, has experienced the consequences of Adam's fatal choice. But today, we more clearly see the devastating results from Eve taking the helm of leadership: the emasculated male. With head bowed low, initiative breathing a raspy death-rattle, men are not only stepping away from leadership, they are slinking away as fast as they can in the opposite direction.

ON THE ONE HAND, WE KNOW THAT AS SONS OF GOD WE HAVE A HIGH AND NOBLE CALLING. ON THE OTHER HAND, WE ARE PAINFULLY AWARE OF OUR FAILURE TO LIVE OUT THAT CALLING CONSISTENTLY.

Janice Shaw Crouse, commenting on how feminism has impacted the American male, says her research indicates that "from a low of just over 19 percent in 1966, the proportion of all men ages 20 to 54 who are unmarried is now more than one-half. Among younger men 20 to 34, more than 70 percent are now unmarried, compared with just under 30 percent in this age group in the mid-1960s at the onset of the sexual revolution."[8]

Men, in growing percentages, are abdicating the role and responsibility of husband. Is it just too hard? Does it require too much? Is chivalry and the desire to serve as one woman's protector and provider completely dead?

Crouse paints a revealing picture of the landscape that has been shaped through feminism's emasculation of the American male:

"Thus, year by year more and more younger men whose biological age should normally predispose them to take up the responsibilities of job, wife and family—activities which build society—are occupying themselves with computer games, pornography, hook-ups and otherwise wasting their potential to contribute and help build a future."[9]

Have men abdicated their responsibilities because they're merely immature, or have they lived under the domination of "brawling women" for so long that they've decided to throw in the towel of commitment and leadership? Men are facing the oppression of muscular feminism on a cultural level, which often mirrors what is occurring in their own home. As you read this next section, keep in mind that, although our culture's views of manhood and womanhood have changed, we as men still have the responsibility to "man up" at home. We can't lay all of the blame on feminism, the current cultural trends, or on our wife's personality—we are responsible to serve our wife as her fearless leader!

Women Who Must Be OBEYED

Have you ever read those verses in Proverbs that deal with the difficult marriage (or the nagging wife)? You know the ones I'm talking about? You probably have them underlined. It's those verses about "leaky roofs" and living in the corner of the house because the wife is . . . well, kind of a witch to live with. Yeah, those are the verses I'm talking about . . .

They put a sympathetic light on the husband and seem to place a harsher light of scrutiny on the wife. Maybe you can identify with, and in a strange way find some kind of comfort in those verses. For example:

"It is better to live in a corner of the housetop than in a house shared with a quarrelsome wife" (Proverbs 21:9, 25:24). Instead of just "quarrelsome" the King James Version of these verses calls the wife a "brawling woman" (just sayin'). Both of these verses use the "corner of the house" imagery and say exactly the same thing—interesting that God saw the need to duplicate this statement!

There's also the "leaky roof" analogy:

"A constant dripping on a day of steady rain and a contentious woman are alike" (Proverbs 27:15 NASB) and "a wife's quarreling is a continual dripping of rain" (Proverbs 19:13). Another version describes this "dripping" as coming through a "leaky roof."

And my personal favorite:

"It is better to live in a desert land than with a contentious and vexing woman" (Proverbs 21:19 NASB). Yep, I've headed to the "desert land" on a few occasions!

Each of these describes what a man will experience when he's in a relationship with a (destructive) fierce woman.

Allow me to break down a few of these for you:

In Proverbs 21:9 and 25:24 we see the husband, outside the house, just trying to get a little space between himself and his difficult wife. Been there? This man feels backed into a corner and escapes to the garage, the golf course, the computer, or pours himself into work to provide a little relief for a short amount of time.

But you always have to come back and face her, and if she knows you've run to the "rooftop" for a break from her—watch out! That only makes things worse.

The wife who is like a "leaky roof" is a constant source of frustration. Her nagging is a continual reminder of your failures—much like a continual dripping rain through a leaky roof that eventually wears away the environment and furnishings of your home, this wife's words will erode your soul.

Finally, there's the picture of the man who has made his choice to leave. He's decided that living in a desert is better than living with this kind of woman. He'd rather face the deprivation of living in a barren wilderness with snakes, lizards, and jackals than to live out the rest of his days with his wife. This man has chosen what you may have fantasized but never acted on.

In each of these verses, the same Hebrew word is used to describe the wife's behavior, whether it's translated "quarrelsome," "contentious," or my personal favorite, "brawling." The word means "to love to fight." The brawling woman is not afraid to "mix it up." She wants to contest almost everything you say or do. Sound familiar?

The key verse to all of these examples is the one that follows the final verse in this series: "A quarrelsome wife is like the dripping of a leaky roof in a rainstorm; restraining her is like restraining the wind or grasping oil with the hand" (Proverbs 27:15–16 NIV). Quite the word picture. When I've tried to restrain my fierce woman, it felt like trying to wrap my arms around a tornado! And if you try to grasp oil, it slides right through your fingers.

You may be ready to quit—because you know that it is literally impossible to "restrain" your "brawling woman." I want to remind you, it will be impossible for you to restrain, change, fix, or remake her. You can't do it. Only God can step into your relationship and do that transforming work. He can speak to the wind and it has to calm. He is able to take the most impossible challenge and grasp it completely, and turn it for our good and His glory.

> **WHEN I'VE TRIED TO RESTRAIN MY FIERCE WOMAN, IT FELT LIKE TRYING TO WRAP MY ARMS AROUND A TORNADO!**

The One who holds both of you in His hand is the only one who can hold your wife. He is your hope. If you run to the desert, you'll never experience the glorious work He can do!

For you brave men who are reading this book, I want to commend you that you've not allowed the culture's devaluation of manhood (or perhaps your wife's emasculating tendencies) to so shut you down that you've given up all attempts to lead your wife. If you had, I don't think you'd still be reading. You've not utterly caved. You still desire to live out the manhood God created you to live. You're still filled with enough hope to pick up this book and read. You (apparently) are still willing to step up to the plate, and again attempt to lead your wife. For that, I commend you.

Rise Up, Man of Faith!

Your wife, your family, your church, needs a man who trusts God and follows Him with unflinching courage. The great need of this hour is men of faith. Men who will dare to believe God. Men who have the courage to stand alone when needed. Men who have the humility to invite other men to come alongside them for accountability and community. Men who go against conventional wisdom because they fully trust in God's wisdom. Men who do not see trusting God as risky. Men of faith, confident in God, His goodness, His power, His faithfulness. Men who say without fear or hesitation "This is what God would have us do—who will join me?"

This was the spirit of Caleb. Remember him? In contrast to the passivity of Adam, Caleb rose up to obey God: "But My servant Caleb, because he has had a different spirit and has followed Me fully, I will bring into the land which he entered, and his descendants shall take possession of it" (Numbers 14:24 NASB).

Caleb saw the same obstacles that the other spies saw. He saw the same giants, the same heavily fortified cities, the same enemies in vast numbers. He saw the same seeming impossibilities. He saw all of this and obviously understood the risk and danger of his mission. So what "different spirit" did Caleb possess that the other spies did not?

His was the courageous faith that pleased God.

All the spies saw the same things, but Caleb saw more than the others. Caleb looked past the impossibilities and he saw God. He believed God. He trusted God. He followed God fully. For Caleb, it wasn't a matter of "seeing" what had to be overcome, but it was a matter of "seeing" what great things God was going to do. Caleb envisioned God getting great glory because of how "impossible" the mission appeared. The others only saw the "impossibility" of attempting what God instructed.

> Then the men who had gone up with him said, "We are not able to go up against the people, for they are stronger than we are." So they brought to the people of Israel a bad report of the land that they had

spied out, saying, "The land, through which we have gone to spy it out, is a land that devours its inhabitants, and all the people that we saw in it are of great height. (Numbers 13:31–32)

Do you feel like your marriage problems are "eating you alive"? Do you fear your wife? Do you think she is "stronger" than you? Better than you? More intelligent or "spiritual" than you? Do you think leading her is an impossible mission? Does she intimidate you? Do you feel inadequate? Have you given up attempting to serve her as her spiritual leader because you've lost all confidence?

Caleb was completely confident in God (v. 30). He said, in effect, "What are we waiting for? Let's go! We have more than enough (God) to ensure victory!"

No matter how dark things seem—you have good reason for hope. God desires to come alongside you in this battle. He wants you to experience victory. The obstacles you've faced in your relationship with your wife may appear as gigantic as the opposition Caleb faced, but are you willing to look beyond what you now see? Are you willing to have faith for what God can do?

Rise up in faith today. Don't let fear weaken you. Trust the God who is able! The same Spirit that was in Caleb dwells in you! Rise up, man of faith!

Listen to the way Theodore Roosevelt challenges us:

It is not the critic that counts . . . who points out how the strong man stumbles or the doer of deeds could have done them better. The credit belongs to the man who is actually in the Arena, whose face is marred by dust and sweat and blood; who strives valiantly; who errs and comes short again and again, because there is no effort without error and shortcoming; but he knows the great devotion; who spends himself in a worthy cause, who at the best, knows in the end the triumph of high achievement, and who at the worst, if he fails while daring greatly, knows that his place shall never be with those cold and timid souls, who know neither victory nor defeat.[10]

Don't let your place be named with the "cold and timid souls, who know neither victory nor defeat." Join me in stepping into the "Arena," in pressing into a valiant battle. In the next chapter, I'll share with you the destructive components that are at work within the man's heart and explain how those tendencies contribute to the "Fierce woman/Fearful man" relationship dynamic. But first, Kim has a closing word for you:

For years, I begged God to give me a spiritual leader. I viewed LeRoy as weak and I'd reached the point in our marriage where I could barely tolerate being in the same room with him. How wrong I was. My perspective drove me to treat him in disrespectful and demeaning ways. But he was no wimp. I wore him down for years, but thankfully, he got back up and began to lead me. He courageously took on his role of spiritual shepherd in our home, and I have the deepest level of love and respect for him today. I pray that, as you bravely begin to live out the truths of Scripture, your wife will respond with newfound admiration and a willingness to follow your lead.

⊰ DIGGING IN ⊱

1. Read through John 11:1–44. The word "disappointed" is never penned in this text, but it is written all over the story. I'm sure Mary and Martha were disappointed. They knew Jesus could have healed their brother. They knew it would be no problem for Him. They told Him as much, as soon as He showed up (four days late, according to them). I can just see Martha's arms crossed and her stern glare as she rebukes Jesus (v. 21). But Jesus didn't drop

His head in shame or allow Martha's rebuke to shut Him down. Instead, He pointed her to the bigger picture. How did Jesus move Martha from a state of rebuking to a state of wonder and faith?

2. What similarities do you see in Caleb's challenge to the spies for faith (Numbers 13:17–33) and Jesus' challenge to Martha?

3. What principles do you see in the examples of Jesus and Caleb that can help you to move your wife beyond the "brawling woman" state to a state of wonder and faith? List those principles and lay out a course of action for that today.

Trapped in the Hurt Locker

There comes into the life of every man a task for which
he and he alone is uniquely suited. What a shame if that moment
finds him either unwilling or unprepared for that which
would become his finest hour [1]

WINSTON CHURCHILL

The gravel crunched hard under my feet as I made the long walk down the hill, then farther down a hidden lane to the small logistics yard. The early morning hour yielded no daylight, but I could still make out the lettering at the entrance to the lane: "Dead End."

Dead End—that's where my life was now headed. I'd walked away from a successful ministry position in a large church, serving as senior pastor while only thirty-one. It was a dream opportunity, and I was only one year into it when I knew I had to resign. I could no longer preach the gospel I'd held so dearly, but now was struggling to believe. I'd prayed for years for God to intervene, for Him to work some kind of miracle in our marriage, but the heavens were silent. I'd seen no change; in fact, things were getting worse.

I could no longer be a man of integrity and preach every Sunday, when inside I was dying. So I left my calling, walked away from pastoring, and settled into the rigorous lifestyle of the eighteen-wheel-over-the-road truck driver, working for my father-in-law's company and living in a small mobile home on the property connected to the truck yard. I would travel sometimes for weeks at a time—the cab of my truck my only refuge. I had retreated to the hurt locker with no hope of escape.

The "hurt locker" is a metaphorical place one goes to after, or while, experiencing defeat, harm, or distress. The phrase is used by the military as slang to describe serious or incapacitating injury. It's a place of suffering.

In the darkest years of our marriage, while trapped in the "hurt locker," I remember crying out to God on a regular basis. Asking Him for answers, asking for help, for relief, for some kind of miracle . . . and getting no response. I wondered where God was in all of the pain. It brought me to a crisis of faith. I began to wonder if God was even listening or if He could possibly care, and eventually questioning if He was there at all. No matter how much I prayed, things only got worse.

What I didn't realize until later, was that Kim was praying in similar ways at the same time. She was crying out to God for answers, she was suffering and enduring long years in her own hurt locker. We both wanted to find a way out of the darkness and confusion, but neither of us understood how to break the cycle of pain and injury. We were caught in a deadly spiral and saw no hope for the future.

Spinning Out of Control

Experienced pilots will tell you that inverted spins—or worse yet, inverted flat spins—are usually unrecoverable. If you get caught in a flat spin, and can't pull out of it, your rapid descent will take the plane nose-down to a fatal crash. That's what we felt was happening.

We were spinning out of control. We felt trapped. We were committed to remaining married, but the marriage was miserable and the future looked hopeless. Neither of us believed we could divorce—it was only our personal commitment to Christ that held us intact. Even though we were dealing with personal fears and doubts in our relationship with Christ, we still held to the truth of His Word and believed we had no valid justification to divorce. We weren't willing to walk away from the marriage (legally), but each of us had long ago walked away from the relationship emotionally. We shared the same roof, but not the same heart.

We tolerated each other at times, but primarily we shared a simmering resentment toward one another. We could spend hours in a car together without ever speaking a word. We rarely enjoyed physical contact. My appetite for that was gone. I felt like a failure in every area. And although it took me several years to realize it—I feared my wife. It's hard to cuddle with a woman you fear.

My resentment toward her grew as I shifted the blame for all of our problems to her. I was a good guy. I was faithful to her. I provided for her. I wasn't running around on her or blowing money on myself. Why couldn't she appreciate me? I was doing the best I could—but it was never good enough!

Any of that sound familiar?

It would be a few more years before any hint of understanding began to crack the destructive

WE SHARED THE SAME ROOF, BUT NOT THE SAME HEART.

cycle of pain, but when God began moving our hearts through a process of conviction and repentance, He provided the key to opening the hurt locker. The first steps out of the cycle began with Kim getting away for several days, and although she didn't plan for it—God showed up. I've asked her to share that part of our journey with you.

ESCAPING THE HURT LOCKER

(Kim): My plan was to run. I told LeRoy I just needed to get away to spend some time alone writing a Bible study for the women in our church, but in my heart I was running. I was sick of how our relationship was going and felt like I couldn't take it anymore. I felt like something had to give. God was going to have to bring an answer or I didn't think I could stand the pain any longer. I took off to a secluded cabin and was only there a few hours when I found a small booklet tucked inside my Bible cover. I didn't even know it was there, but I came across it while looking for something else. I pulled it out and started reading.

The booklet contained several Scriptures and diagnostic questions that took me on a personal journey of introspection . . . the Holy Spirit leading the way. The Scriptures were not new to me, I'd read them many times, the difference was that God met with me in that quiet place and opened my eyes to how He viewed me in relation to how I was living out "womanhood."

God used questions like:

"In the way I talk to and about men, do I show them their God-created worth and value?"

"Do I make it easy for men to fulfill their God-given calling to lead in the home, the church, and the society?"

"Do I respond to men in ways that communicate appropriate respect and affirmation of their manhood?"

I had to answer "No" to all three of those questions.

There was more:

"Do I bless my family, friends, and acquaintances by speaking words that are kind and wise?"

"Do I seek to influence others by means of gentle words, rather than controlling or intimidating them with harsh words?"[2]

If LeRoy had hammered me with questions like these, I would've come out swinging or put up a defensive front, but in a quiet and gentle way the Holy Spirit began to peel back layers of pride. It was a gracious work of God. It was answered prayer.

You may be reading this and thinking, "I've got to get that book for my wife!" And that may be a good option . . . but before you push the book in her face, let me challenge you to seek God first. The work He did in my life (I now believe) was in great part due to a man of God (my husband) who set his heart to seek God in prayer. God changed my heart, but it may be that God wants to change your heart first, before He will do that work in your wife. I wasn't the only one who needed a heart-change; LeRoy will tell you that he did as well. But see, the problem was that when we were both trapped in the hurt locker, both of us were finger-pointing and blaming the other for all the pain and problems. We equally believed we were justified in our anger and resentment. God had to start bringing down those walls.

Once I humbled myself before God and started taking responsibility for my part in our marital misery, God began opening my eyes to more and more junk that I'd never seen. After spending several days under conviction, and writing out lengthy pages of confession, I asked to meet with LeRoy.

Honestly, although I'd always considered myself a strong woman, I was scared to death to tell him that I now realized how wrong I was and ask him to forgive me. I really thought he would take advantage of me, and somehow "make me pay" for the years of pain. I fought hard to resist asking his forgiveness, but I couldn't escape the Holy Spirit's conviction. I couldn't go back to life as it had been. I was determined to walk out of the hurt locker, no matter how hard it was to take the necessary steps to leave.

In brokenness, I poured out to him how wrong I'd been—for years—in how I treated him. I asked him to read the notebook full of pages that I'd saturated with reams of confession and tears, and then I asked for his forgiveness.

LeRoy's reaction surprised me. He didn't show much emotion. There was no hint that he was planning revenge, but there also wasn't a big celebration or show of relief. He just sat there with the same blank stare that characterized much of our marriage. His hope had died, and my admission and repentance weren't affecting him one bit. But even in the wake of his "non-reaction" I knew that I wasn't turning back. I'd escaped the hurt locker and I was determined to never return.

(LeRoy): When Kim poured out her heart to me, I couldn't really grasp the importance of what was happening. I was suspicious. I didn't know how long her "repentance" would last. I was so spent, so tired of trying and failing, so deep into my own cave of depression that her appeal for forgiveness couldn't even reach my heart. I had lost all hope and even her broken condition didn't faze me. I was done.

What I didn't realize right away, but have learned since, was that Kim's fierceness wasn't the whole problem in our relationship. She wasn't the sole contributor to our problems. The day she came and asked my forgiveness, she seemed to think it was all her fault. And I guess I did too at that point. But really, you and I both know that it is never only one person's fault when there are marriage problems. I just didn't realize my own issues until much later.

But that's why I'm sharing my story with you. I don't want you to stay trapped in the hurt locker as long as I was. I want to let you know what I've learned. And since you've picked up this book, I have a feeling that your wife hasn't had a "Come to Jesus" event like my wife did, and it may be that God is requiring you to open your heart first, to lead your wife in the escape from the hurt locker.

Battling the Big Three

As we began rebuilding our relationship, I came to realize that there are three heart issues that I struggled with, and I believe are common to most men. In this chapter, I want to talk with you about those destructive tendencies and challenge you to be open to what God may want to show you. These heart issues can manifest themselves in different ways according to a man's particular temperament or behavioral patterns, so the way I reacted to a heart issue like "pride" or "ingratitude" may look different than how it crops up in your life. But once you begin recognizing the source of sinful manifestations by tracing them back to the root issue, you can go to battle to eradicate that mess.

In *Fierce Women*, Kim distilled the destructive components that fuel the "Fierce Woman/Fearful Man" cycle down to three basic heart issues: Pride, Ingratitude, and Fear. And you know, as we've grappled with our relationship issues, we've discovered that men are plagued by those same three heart issues. They just express them differently. With women, all three of those components work in tandem and erupt in the desire to control the man.

For men, those three heart issues can result in developing a lifestyle in relating to the wife in two extremes: Passivity or Domination. In this chapter, we're going to zero in on each of these three destructive components and hopefully this will help you to recognize them when they show up in your relationship with your wife:

Fear: **False Evidence Appearing Real**
Ingratitude: **The Demand for "MORE!"**
Pride: **It's All about Me!**

I want you to be prepared so that you can run into the battle with confidence. Men, this could be "your finest hour" as you willingly throw yourself into a time of intensive training for this battle. This chapter will help you identify the heart issues you're struggling with and in the next chapter we'll investigate how to battle those issues. Don't get discouraged if you see things in your heart that you haven't realized were there. Having an eye-opening wake-up call is necessary if you want to get out of the hurt locker. Don't miss out on what God wants to show you in these next few pages.

God's Most Significant Question

Let's return to that garden. In order to understand the present, your situation and mine, we need to look to the past. After Adam's fatal fall, he and his wife were hiding in the bushes. They were naked, fearful, and ashamed when God approached the man with a very important question:

"But the Lord God called to the man and said to him, 'Where are you?'" (Genesis 3:9).

It is significant that God asks Adam "Where are you?" not "What have you done?" or "What have you failed to do?" He doesn't ask him, "Where have you been? What did you have for lunch?" But God pinpointed His heart-search by asking the man, "Where are you?"

Eve was the one who first gave way to Satan's temptation—but notice that God didn't address her, He went directly to Adam. He wanted to know where Adam was at that moment, not what had happened or what led up to that moment, but asked pointedly, "Where are you—right now?"

God operates in the eternal present and just as it was with Adam, so it is with us now. The question is forever in the present tense to every son of Adam. "Where are you?" Not "Where is your wife?" Not "Where is your marriage?" But God asks, "Where are *you*?"

God, of course, knew Adam's "GPS" coordinates. God knew where Adam was geographically, but more importantly, God knew that

Adam's spiritual condition was a result of his fall to temptation. God also knew the consequences that were unknown (at this point) to Adam. So, God wasn't asking for information, but issued the question as a confrontation to Adam's heart issues.

The question lingers in the air still, not only for Adam but for all of us under sin's curse. God's question remains unchanged by the passage of time. Just as it was spoken in the garden, it clearly sounds out to you wherever you are at this moment. Consider that question, "Where are you?" as we walk through these root heart issues. The first heart issue is the one I've struggled with most, not just in my marriage, but throughout my life.

Fear: False Evidence Appearing Real

The first manifestation of fear in human history comes from a man. After the woman eats from the forbidden fruit, the man follows her lead. Was he afraid to confront the serpent and tell him to get out of his garden? Was he afraid to take a stand with Eve and direct her away from the tree? The text doesn't provide those answers, but what we do see is the man grabbing fig leaves to invent some sort of "covering" for his naked body, while hiding in the bushes from his Creator.

> And they heard the sound of the Lord God walking in the garden in the cool of the day, and the man and his wife hid themselves from the presence of the Lord God among the trees of the garden. But the Lord God called to the man and said to him, "Where are you?" And he said, "I heard the sound of you in the garden, and I was afraid, because I was naked, and I hid myself." (Genesis 3:8–10)

Did the first couple fear that they were missing out on something they "deserved?" Did they fear that the Creator may not be looking out for their best interest after all—by withholding this fruit? Did they fear that He may have lied to them?

ONE OF THE LESSONS GOD TAUGHT ME DURING THE DARKEST DAYS OF OUR MARRIAGE WAS THAT A FEARFUL MAN CANNOT BE A FAITHFUL MAN.

Fear distorts and perverts reality. It takes false accusations and presents them as reality. Fear seems to be the enemy's favorite weapon in his arsenal. But there is a fear that conquers the enemy's terrorizing attacks. Fear of God, properly formed in our minds and hearts, provides the courage to live without fear of anyone or anything else. An accurate view of God results in an awe and reverential fear that will be our protection against every assault of the evil one.

One of the many lessons God taught me during the darkest days of our marriage was that a fearful man cannot be a faithful man. From the outside, I looked like a faithful husband, faithful father, faithful pastor, and I was those things—externally. But internally, I was a fearful husband, fearful father, and a fearful pastor. I was afraid to lead spiritually. I was afraid of failing as a parent. I was afraid of disappointing everyone in my life.

So I hid.

I hid in my cave of depression. I hid from making decisions for fear of failure. I hid from God while still seeking God. My heart was a dark, gloomy place where fear was like a thick fog, obscuring the truths that I knew about God. I was immobilized by fear most of the time, losing all hope that anything would ever change. At other times, I could function quite normally, but the fear was always there lurking in the shadows of my heart.

You may not think you're a fearful man. It took me a long time to recognize that I was, and even longer to admit it. But I hope you'll consider God's question "Where are you?" as you walk through the indicators I've listed below:

Indicators of Fear:

* Having the tendency to retreat or run from relational interaction, especially when there is potential for conflict
* Thoughts permeated with "What ifs"
* Frequently suspicious and paranoid of others
* Primarily having a negative outlook on life
* Dreading social interaction
* Blame shifting
* Falsifying or exaggerating facts in order to protect yourself or impress others
* Unwilling to take "risks" or venture into the unknown
* Delaying making decisions for fear of potential failure
* Laziness from fear of failure
* Taking shortcuts rather than making hard choices
* Neglecting to pray with your wife or demonstrate spiritual leadership

I hope that list didn't totally shut you down or demoralize you. That's not my purpose in having you walk through it. I'm being gut-level honest with you because I know if you're in the hurt locker, there's a good chance that you've been paralyzed by fear for a long time. I've been there, and I don't want you to stay there. And I'm here to assure you that you don't have to stay there.

This chapter's purpose is to help us get a better picture of the three primary heart issues that may be contributing to your marital problems. We won't look into a battle plan for dealing with these issues until the next chapter, so hang in here with me. Don't get discouraged if you recognize yourself in any of these lists. It's to be expected that you'll see some tendencies, but my hope is that rather than shutting down, you'll man up to admit where you are and come clean with God so that He can lead you out of that hurt locker!

Ingratitude: The Demand for "MORE!"

God placed within us a desire for "More." "More" in the sense of not being satisfied with less than what He created us for. A craving for "More" is a good craving, an urge to go beyond; a holy dissatisfaction; a yearning for the glorious heights and the challenges of pushing the envelope. It's that stirring you feel at the end of the last play of the Final Four when "One Shining Moment" blares through the scenes of the greatest plays of March Madness. The desire for "More" can be a good thing. Or it can become our corruption.

THE FIRST COUPLE COVETED WHAT THEY COULD NOT HAVE.

> The Lord God took the man and put him in the Garden of Eden to work it and keep it. And the Lord God commanded the man, saying, "You may surely eat of every tree of the garden, but of the tree of the knowledge of good and evil you shall not eat, for in the day that you eat of it you shall surely die." (Genesis 2:15–17)

You would think while living in paradise, having an overabundance of goodness and pleasure at your fingertips, that you would be content. But, no, the first couple coveted what they could not have. Eve went for it first, but Adam could've led her away from the temptation. He could've taken a stand and confronted the serpent. But he took the forbidden fruit and ate with his wife.

The lure of the forbidden is answered by the last commandment of the ten God gave to Moses on Mount Sinai: "You shall not covet . . ." (Exodus 20:17). Adam and Eve wanted MORE! They wanted what was not theirs to take. At the heart of their disobedience was a lack of gratitude for all God's good gifts.

As a pastor, one thing I've observed in counseling people who are living an immoral lifestyle, whether it is porn addiction or immoral sexual activity, is that immoral people are ungrateful people. Nancy

DeMoss Wolgemuth makes the connection between ingratitude and immorality in her book *Choosing Gratitude: Your Journey to Joy:*

> Ungrateful people are bent on gratifying themselves. They tend to focus on "my needs," "my hurts," "my feelings," "my desires," "how I have been treated, neglected, failed, or wounded." An unthankful person is full of himself, seldom pausing to consider the needs and feelings of others.
>
> Incidentally, I believe this is why a common end result of ingratitude is the sin of moral impurity. A person who is wrapped up in herself, whose whole world revolves around getting her own needs met, is prime bait for a tempter who thrives on accusing God of being unfair and ungenerous. An ungrateful heart is quick to notice when self is feeling unsatisfied, and is vulnerable to resorting to sinful acts and behaviors in an attempt to eliminate pain and experience personal pleasure.[3]

Ingratitude develops unhealthy and addictive cravings. When we first answer the call to an attractive offer to fulfill a craving, or think we've found the object that will finally satisfy our desires, we're usually unaware of the enslaving cords of bondage as they begin wrapping round our hearts and minds. Consider the following descriptions and ask the Holy Spirit to alert you through these lists to anything in your life that might have the potential to be a fleshly addiction.

Desires That Enslave:
* Spring from self-centered thoughts and motives
* Are shrouded in secrecy or fulfilled under cover of darkness
* Can lead to crossing lines that expand far beyond God's clear direction
* Carry with them the fear of being caught while gratifying them

* Have an addictive pull
* Require layers of justification based on your "unique" situation or need
* Are "all about me"
* Prevent sincere worship

Gratification of These Desires:

* Involves anything that is morally corrupt, spiritually perverted, and is physically harmful or addictive
* Leaves you with feelings of guilt and shame, but always hungry for more
* Ultimately brings harm to others

In contrast to the desires of the flesh and the destruction they produce, Galatians 5 describes the fruit produced by the desires of the Spirit: "love, joy, peace, patience, kindness, goodness, faithfulness, gentleness, self-control . . ."[4]

> INGRATITUDE IS NOT ONLY A FAILURE TO BE THANKFUL FOR WHAT YOU HAVE, BUT IT BLAMES GOD FOR WHAT HE HAS GIVEN YOU.

When God confronted Adam with his sin, and point-blank asked him, "Have you eaten of the tree of which I commanded you not to eat?" (Genesis 3:11). The man's response reveals his ingratitude. He shifts blame to the woman and even to God. "The man said, 'The woman whom you gave to be with me, she gave me fruit of the tree . . .'" (Genesis 3:12).

No longer is the man grateful for God's gift of his soul mate and companion, but now he lashes out at God and throws his woman under the bus. Ingratitude is not only a failure to be thankful for what you have, but it blames God for what He has given you. It accuses God of injustice and ineptitude. Ingratitude attributes culpability to God as the source of your sorrow. Ingratitude leads to coveting, immorality, greed, justification of sin, bitterness, blame shifting, and selfishness. Ingratitude is often the underlying and less discernible culprit of relationship conflicts.

Ingratitude showed up in our relationship when I believed I deserved to be treated better; when I thought about what a good guy I was, and how much I was "sacrificing." When it seemed my efforts were never good enough, I let resentment build toward Kim. Ingratitude covets what you don't have, and I was coveting appreciation.

I felt unappreciated by Kim, was hurt and offended, and I certainly wasn't thankful for her, for our marriage, for pretty much anything that was happening in my life during those dark years. I coveted peace and quiet. I craved comfort. But those things were in short supply at home. And I'm ashamed to say that when Kim wanted to "discuss" emotional issues, gratitude for her was the last thing on my mind . . . I just wanted solitude. I just wanted to be left alone.

You may not think you're an ungrateful man. I didn't. And most of you may already be at a low point, struggling under a load of guilt and feeling like a failure, so my intention isn't to bury you further, but to help you to recognize heart issues that could be contributors to your marital misery. I encourage you to carefully walk through this list of indicators with a receptive heart and ask God to open your eyes to recognize yourself if you're guilty of any of these:

Indicators of Ingratitude:

* Believing you're getting a raw deal; consistently thinking you deserve better treatment
* Frequently complaining; grumbling about circumstances
* Having a negative and critical spirit

* Being discontent; never satisfied
* Frequently experiencing resentment, bitterness, and anger
* Obsessing over what you don't have
* Coveting what others have
* Assuming either an entitlement or a victim mentality

As you read through that list, what is your response to God's question: "Where are you?"

Until we realize the seriousness of our own sin, we stand as a hindrance to God working in our marriage. If all we can see is our wife's sin or failures, then we are not in a position for God to hear or respond to our prayers. We must see our own sin in the full light of God's holiness.

Pride: The Rebel Within

My dad is a real "man's man." He doesn't mind telling you that he's a rebel. He proudly admits his stubbornness and wears it as a badge of honor. My dad grew up in an era when the world's issues were settled in broad strokes of black and white. No matter the era when we were born, we're all born with a proud heart. All of us.

Pride is the spiritual cancer of us all.

Pride is what drives us to function independently of God.

I never thought of myself as a proud man. But pride was a primary driving force in my life as I shut down and went to my cave for safety. Five years into our marriage, I was already struggling with depression and feeling trapped by marriage. When I confided my struggle to one of my theology professors, his solution was a kind of "John Wayne" approach. He told me I just needed to "man up" and "pull myself up by my bootstraps" and tell my wife she needed to think and talk less. Right. That would've gone over real well. After that conversation, I slipped even further into the pit.

The answer to our pride problem isn't exhibiting more pride. The answer to our pride problem isn't looking to ourselves for rescue. The answer to our pride problem is NOT pulling ourselves up by our own "bootstraps."

Adam's pride is evident in his response to God's confrontation:

> But the Lord God called to the man and said to him, "Where are you?" And he said, "I heard the sound of you in the garden, and I was afraid, because I was naked, and I hid myself." He said, "Who told you that you were naked? Have you eaten of the tree of which I commanded you not to eat?" (Genesis 3:9–11)

For the first time, Adam makes a choice that separates him from God. He has a new "self-awareness" and is filled with shame. Adam declares his state of being: naked. Adam's man-centered view replaces his God-centered view. Adam's sinful condition has turned his eyes from God to himself. This causes Adam to take matters into his own hands to solve his newfound problem. Adam begins acting in pride, rather than humility. And what he doesn't yet realize is that humility is the pathway to the heart of God.

Humility before God does not come from beating yourself down, taking on a self-deprecating attitude that is demeaning, but humility flows from having a right view of God, which then results in a right view of yourself.

It is an interesting question that God asks of Adam at this point. "Who told you that you were naked?" God is challenging Adam to consider how he reached his point of self-awareness. The question highlights the source that Adam is depending on for his understanding of his personhood. He's chosen to function independently from God.

You are probably hearing a lot of voices in your head telling you negative things about who you are, defining your personhood and identity. But it is a dangerous thing to listen to condemning messages, because they aren't from God. Are you believing that you're a loser? Can never do anything right? Aren't able to be a courageous leader?

The condemning voices in your head may come from guilt over your sin—and that is something that must be confessed and acknowledged before God. God was leading Adam to a point of confession as He challenged him with each question. But, it is important to note that Adam was not only guilty of eating the forbidden fruit, he was guilty of listening to (and heeding) the wrong voices. He listened to Eve and ate. He listened to the voices of shame in his head and hid. He pointed to Eve as the reason to justify his sin and he blamed God.

We can be humbled by our difficult circumstances (a miserable marriage, a dead-end job), but when we're in the midst of those hard places and we continue to cling to a defensive posture, that is an indicator that we are still functioning in pride. In the book of Job, we see a man crushed by the cruel aspects of life in a fallen world: loss of health, loss of property, loss of family (plus the "encouragement" from a wife who wished him dead). He was experiencing significant crushing, but throughout most of the book, Job functions in defensive mode. It wasn't until he finally came to the end of himself and repented of his heart condition that God was then able to step in and work in his life (Job 42:6).

Indicators of Pride:

- ❋ Self-concern
- ❋ Self-exaltation
- ❋ Defensiveness
- ❋ Easily offended
- ❋ Unwilling to consider an opposing viewpoint
- ❋ Not teachable

* Blind to personal weaknesses
* Stubborn
* Controlling
* Craving praise from others
* Insecurity stemming from concern over others' opinion of you
* Fear of man
* Self-pity

As you read through that list, what is your response to God's question: "Where are you?"

Pride strings us along, carrying us away from repentance. Adam delayed repenting. Job delayed repenting. When there is no genuine repentance, pride is the culprit. And what if your pride is preventing the work of grace God wants to bring into your life?

As we've taken a hard look at these destructive components, have you been stirred? Have you recognized any of these same sinful tendencies residing in your heart? Will you consider your need to repent?

Are you ready to chuck this book? Go ahead, toss it. But if you do, you may never know the goodness that God has stored up for you. I'm a living testimony to the fact that God has some good stuff, really good stuff, ahead. I wanted to die at times, even figured out how I could do it, but God rescued me and He can do the same for you. I encourage you to spend some time asking God where He finds you today and what He'd have you do.

Ready to step out of that hurt locker?

> **PRIDE STRINGS US ALONG, CARRYING US AWAY FROM REPENTANCE.**

⊰ DIGGING IN ⊱

1. Spend some time investigating Jesus in Philippians 2:5–11. We are challenged to have this same mindset that He had when He chose to take on the form of a servant. What kind of transition did that require? How does His humility affect you?

2. Taking on the mindset of Christ will allow you to live out the command of Philippians 2:4. What is that command? How would you apply this verse to your relationship with your wife?

3. God humbling Himself is an amazing paradox. If you are in any way functioning in pride, sinful fear, or ingratitude—are you willing to humble yourself and confess the specific ways you are doing this?

Run into the Battle

Every soldier must know, before he goes into battle, how the little
battle he is to fight fits into the larger picture, and how the success of
his fighting will influence the battle as a whole.[1]

BERNARD LAW MONTGOMERY
*(the "Spartan General" of the British Army and one of
the heroes of World War II)*

Kristin's tears fell as she listened to Kim and I share how God
transformed our marriage. Kristin reached out to us after
she heard a radio interview because she was struggling
with guilt. Guilt, because Kristin's marriage story ended much differently than ours. Her gifted husband, loved by all who knew him,
chose to end his life. As Kristin listened to our story, she recognized
herself. She relived the painful years of struggle and wondered what
life might have held, if only she'd responded to him differently. We
assured Kristin that, although she had regrets and made choices that
contributed to the destructive cycle in their relationship, she was

not responsible for her husband's fatal choice. I didn't know her husband, but I (LeRoy) could relate to his desire to escape.

There were days when suicide seemed the best option.

I don't know where you are right now. I don't know exactly what your thoughts have been. Only God knows those most jagged edges of your pain. But, if your marriage is anything like ours at its worst point, I have a pretty good idea of where your mind often goes. It is difficult to come out and admit my darkest moments publicly, but I'm willing to confess this to you, so that you'll know that you're not alone in what you feel. I was there, overwhelmed by despair, hopelessness, feeling abandoned by God . . . and desiring a way out, longing for death. And I'm ashamed of what I'm about to admit to you.

There were many times in the darkest season of our marriage misery, while trying to sort out the pain in my heart and the torment in my mind, when I fantasized about ending the hopelessness. I was convinced it would be the best thing for Kim. The best thing for both of us. I shudder as I write this, but I have to tell you the truth. I wanted to die and I was ready to take that step into my own hands.

While driving, I wanted to straighten out a curve and leave the road, to fly off a steep embankment to a (hopefully) sudden death. I fantasized about it often. But then, I figured that carbon monoxide would be the more reliable option. Sometimes when I was in a dangerous work situation, I would silently hope that something might go wrong and it would all be over, an "accident" would end it all. No more pain.

AFTER A PARTICULARLY EMOTIONAL AND HUMILIATING EXCHANGE WITH KIM, I SIMPLY WALKED AWAY. AND KEPT WALKING.

Can you relate?

I'm ashamed to tell you that I also was tempted to abandon Kim. Just run away, change my name, I could live as a vagabond, drop off the face of the earth—anything would be preferable to how we were living. After a particularly emotional and humiliating exchange with Kim, where once again I could not counter her intensity, answer her arguments, defend my position, calm her composure, or deescalate the situation, I simply walked away. And kept walking. I walked into some thick woods and stayed there for hours. I didn't want to ever leave. I just wanted to stay there and die of starvation or exposure at the base of a lonely oak. Pathetic, I know.

Suicide is putting the "victim" in control. And after being held under your wife's control for an extended period of time, gaining any control at all is a huge temptation. It's like the final big retaliation against the person who has hurt you the most. Thankfully, God's grace protected me from my sinful desires. I never acted on those fantasies. I didn't want to die a coward, or die putting myself before others. I couldn't do that to our children, but in a twisted way, I believed that others would be better off without me. Kim would, for sure (my warped thinking had convinced me of that lie). But what ultimately protected me from acting on my sick plans was that I didn't want to dishonor the testimony of Christ. In my mind, I could justify my sin of suicide, but in my heart, I couldn't justify bringing shame to my Lord.

I don't know where you are as you read these words, but listen to me. I would have missed out on so much good stuff that God had in store for me if I had checked out twenty-five years ago. I would have brought such heartache and pain, but ultimately, I would've destroyed my gospel witness. The thief who comes to steal, kill, and destroy would've been delighted (John 10:10). But thankfully, God had a better plan. He rescued us.

But that rescue plan involved many small battles along the way. We want to help you recognize how you can "run into" your personal battles in order to win the victory in your marriage. In the last chapter, Kim and I shared with you three primary heart issues that we see affecting marriages today:

Fear: **False Evidence Appearing Real**
Ingratitude: **The Demand for "MORE!"**
Pride: **It's All About Me!**

In contrast to those destructive tendencies, in this chapter, we want to give you a battle plan for recognizing and dealing with those heart issues:

Love: **The Fruit Born from Dying to Self**
Humility: **The Response of a True View of God**
Grace: **God's Empowering Response to Humility**

I started off this chapter by sharing with you the powerful lure of suicide. When your life is controlled by fear to such an extent that you believe the only answer is self-annihilation, then it's time to die. No, I don't mean that it's time to commit suicide—that's never the right answer—I mean it's time to die. Die to your selfishness. Die to your self-protection. Die to your fear of your wife. It's time to die. In order to conquer fear, you're going to need to die.

Love: The Fruit Born from Dying to Self

As men, we take pride in the idea that we would take a bullet for our wives or loved ones. We'd gladly rush into the battle to save the damsel in distress, or fight for our country's liberties, we'd rush into traffic and risk death to save a wandering toddler . . . but I rarely hear men talking about the most heroic form of death, and really the starting point for courage: death to me.

Death to self is the message of the New Testament, but it's easy to turn a deaf ear or let our eyes glaze over when we come to those passages. But consider this: What if the problem in your marriage isn't your wife's fierceness but actually is your unwillingness to die? What if you're the kind of big-talking man that brags you'll take a bullet for her, but you won't even lay down your life in the scriptural way in order to love her? Do you even know what the definition of love is, according to God?

"By this we know love, that he laid down his life for us, and we ought to lay down our lives for the brothers" (1 John 3:16).

Did you skip that verse? Read it again, and when you get to the words "the brothers" insert your wife's name. When you get to the words "we ought to lay down our lives" replace that with "I ought to lay down my life."

You may be scared to death of your wife (and never admitted that—even to yourself), but the answer to dealing with that fear isn't pulling yourself up by your bootstraps, or even picking up a motivational read on self-esteem. No, the real answer to your fear is to truly love your wife:

"There is no fear in love, but perfect love casts out fear. For fear has to do with punishment, and whoever fears has not been perfected in love" (1 John 4:18).

And you know the type of love that Scripture says you're to show your wife? It's the die-to-self love that Jesus showed you on the cross. In fact, you can't love your wife until you die. Just as Jesus' sacrifice provides us with protection, our self-sacrifice is to provide protection for our wives.

We'll talk about practical ways to flesh out sacrificial love to our wives when we get to the "P-R-O-T-E-C-T-I-O-N" acronym in the next chapters, but right now I want to challenge you to adopt a mindset, really a determination, to actually demonstrate love. And I'm not even challenging you to show love to your wife first, I'm asking you to consider: Do you really love Jesus?

Jesus summed up our life mission with these words:

But when the Pharisees heard that he had silenced the Sadducees, they gathered together. And one of them, a lawyer, asked him a question to test him. "Teacher, which is the great commandment in the Law?" And he said to him, "You shall love the Lord your God with all your heart and with all your soul and with all your mind. This is the great and first commandment. And a second is like it: You shall love your neighbor as yourself. On these two commandments depend all the Law and the Prophets." (Matthew 22:34–40)

We can only love our wives when our love for Christ increases to such an extent that our love for God overflows into a love for others. And "others" includes your wife. When you love your wife, it is out of your love for Christ that love for her happens. If you're not loving your wife, then you really aren't loving Christ.

I can hear you now. "You don't know my wife!" No, I don't. But I know my wife. And I know that I felt like she was impossible to love—mainly because she scared me to death!

But fear is conquered through love.

When I first met my wife, I "fell" in love. But really—I didn't have a clue. I told my wife, "I love you," before I even understood what those words really meant or required. Maybe I told her that hoping to get a kiss. I'm sure I said those words because I thought that I did, but I was indoctrinated with an Americanized twentieth-century concept of love that falls far short of true love.

True love conquers fear because true love isn't focused on protecting itself, but focuses on expending itself. Kim and I eventually realized that "true love" is much different than the selfish version of love we'd seen promoted all our lives. I had to learn that true love actually steps into fear. C. S. Lewis describes the danger of protecting your heart from love:

To love at all is to be vulnerable. Love anything, and your heart will certainly be wrung and possibly broken. If you want to make sure of keeping it intact, you must give your heart to no one, not even to an animal. Wrap it carefully round with hobbies and little luxuries; avoid all entanglements; lock it up safe in the casket or coffin of your selfishness. But in that casket—safe, dark, motionless, airless—it will change. It will not be broken; it will become unbreakable, impenetrable, irredeemable.[2]

True love doesn't promise you a painless existence; in fact, true love invites you to step into death. Remember how Jesus described the greatest love? Let this sink in: "Greater love has no one than this, that someone lay down his life for his friends" (John 15:13). Jesus had every right to say that because Jesus did that. Literally. And He did that for you.

> **THE KIND OF SELF-DEATH I'M DESCRIBING IS NOT A ONETIME OCCURRENCE. IT WILL NEED TO BE REPEATED DAILY, EVEN MOMENT-BY-MOMENT.**

Now, don't misunderstand, He doesn't call us to literally die (it is rare that we actually need to save someone's life by sacrificing our own), but He does call us to put our "selves" to death. In order to live out true love a true death is required—the *death* to self. And the kind of self-death I'm describing is not a onetime occurrence. It will need to be repeated daily, even moment-by-moment. This death allows us to live the crucified life described by the apostle Paul:

> I have been crucified with Christ. It is no longer I who live, but Christ who lives in me. And the life I now live in the flesh I live by faith in the Son of God, who loved me and gave himself for me. (Galatians 2:20)

Marriage carries with it daily opportunities for expressing this kind of love in real-life, hard-against-the-grain situations. It can be the greatest sanctifying agent in your life, but in order for sanctification (growth in living out love) to occur, you must be willing to die. Putting to death self-centered agendas, selfish pursuits, self-motivated plans, self-pity, and self-absorption will require laying down your life. And wasn't that the commitment you made when you took your bride by the hand and led her from the wedding altar?

Isn't that the picture that God gives us?

"Husbands, love your wives, as Christ loved the church and gave himself up for her . . ." (Ephesians 5:25).

Have we heard that so many times that our ears have become deaf to it?

Do we think that's too lofty an assignment or an impossible goal?

Loving our wives is not easy. In fact, it's impossible without dying to self.

HOW LOVE AFFECTS THE COURAGEOUS LEADER:

* He responds to the call to follow Christ knowing it requires a painful death—death to self.
* He lays down his life by plunging into the love of Christ.
* He loves God and others with the abandon of the servant warrior who knows no retreat.

At one point, I believed that our marriage was going to be the death of me . . . and I didn't realize it at the time, but that "death of me" was exactly what God wanted. Our marriage wasn't delighting God, our pain wasn't what He wanted for us ultimately, but He knew that's what we needed to bring us to the end of "ourselves." And He brought true resurrection life from that death. He can do that in your marriage as well. I'm challenging you to conquer your fear through love.

Humility: The Response of a True View of God

We saw the destructive component of ingratitude in the last chapter, and you might think that conquering ingratitude comes through being thankful. But actually, thankfulness, or gratitude, is a result of humility. And humility is only possible through having a right view of God. When our view of God is perverted, we no longer humble ourselves in gratitude. We see that expressed in Romans 1:21: "For although they knew God, they did not honor him as God or give thanks to him . . ."

Paul explains that having a warped perspective of God, not honoring Him in His position, not recognizing His authority and right to rule our life, results in an unthankful heart. Paul said that the ungrateful fools "exchanged the glory of the immortal God for images resembling mortal man . . ." (Romans 1:21–23). They failed to recognize or give glory to God as God. In order to experience gratitude, we must recognize God's authority and trustworthy character, but we will not be able to see that when our eyes are focused on ourselves and on our pain.

Humility shifts our focus from self to God.

Humility gets a bad rap today. People have confused humility with unhealthy debasement. Humility is not having a negative self-image. No, not at all, in fact . . . humility's view of self is eclipsed by a right view of God. In reality, humility has little to do with how I see myself, but has everything to do with how I see God. Humility is the heart's response to a proper view of God.

Humility is not beating yourself up or submitting to abusive behavior. And yes, some of you guys are going through some abuse—verbally, and maybe even physically! I'm not dismissing or ignoring that, we'll get to how to deal with that as we work our way through the next chapters, but before we address how to deal with your wife's sinful behavior, we must establish where your heart is.

Do you have a grateful heart?

In our darkest days, the last thing I would have thought about myself was that I was filled with ingratitude. But actually, not only was I ungrateful, I was harboring bitterness toward my wife and worst of all—bitterness toward my God. Although I didn't realize it, I was repeating the complaint Adam expressed to God after the fall:

"The man said, 'The woman whom *you* gave to be with me, she gave me fruit of the tree, and I ate'" (Genesis 3:12, emphasis mine).

This primordial seed of ingratitude is the sinful source of all of men's sour bitterness toward their wife. If I had only one word to challenge men with, it would be this word: bitterness. When men fear their wives, are convinced that they can do nothing to please their wives, or think they deserve better treatment, their resentment grows. It grows until it festers into a bitter root, like an abscessed tooth.

In forty years of ministry, I've never encountered a person trapped in a sinful behavior or lifestyle who had a grateful heart. Without exception, all who were involved in destructive behavior had either an obvious, or a hidden, root of bitterness.

"Mr. O." was an elderly man who wore bitterness on his face, bore it in his sagging shoulders, and carried it in his harsh tone of voice. He was a proud man. He was proud of his accomplishments, his home, his military service, his moderate wealth. But he was bitter. He had an abundance of things to be thankful for: a loving and kind wife, prosperity, and good health, but he had few friends. His bitterness was toxic and people couldn't stand to be around him. There was only a small handful at his funeral. Bitterness will define a life, and if a man doesn't allow the gospel to do its work to tear out that root, bitterness will take a man to a lonely grave.

The Scripture simply states, "Love your wives," but we cannot love them while being ungrateful for them. We cannot love them without thanking God for them. That's why Paul frames his injunction to husbands in Colossians with thankfulness.[3]

You cannot be thankful for your wife and bitter toward her at the same time. It's not possible. It would be like a guy saying he is both a devoted Yankees fan while also passionate about their hated rival—the Red Sox. Impossible. Not happening. For you to be thankful for your wife, when it seems that she is the primary reason for life's misery, is going to require humility.

Humility is a fruit of dying to self—which births gratitude. It's the type of humility that allows the stripping away of everything, dying completely to self . . . but that isn't where it ends. After death comes the resurrection . . . the resurrection power of Christ at work in your life bringing hope, trust, and faith. True humility and gratitude for what God has done for you will wash away all ingratitude.

HOW HUMILITY AFFECTS THE COURAGEOUS LEADER:

* He recognizes God is God and he's not, so he can surrender completely to Him.
* He is willing to confess his need for God and confess his sin.
* Because he recognizes God's worth and value, he is able to walk humbly before Him and treat others with kindness and respect.
* He walks in repentance and easily offers forgiveness to others.
* His humility births gratitude, which destroys bitterness.
* He's teachable and open to counsel for spiritual growth from others. He's willing to be held accountable after being confronted with blindspots.
* His strength is not diminished by humility but is refined and tempered by it.

Gratitude will affect your perspective on everything from your finances to your sexual activities. If you are having frequent conflicts in these areas, before blaming your wife, evaluate your level of gratitude. Practical solutions will never help solve those conflicts if you're filled with ingratitude.

LeRoy didn't realize that he was ungrateful, but his bitterness toward me (Kim) was obvious, and that bitterness stirred a deep resentment in me toward him. We were creating a toxic environment in our home. There would be days that I was determined to bathe him with love and kindness, and his bitterness would shut me down in the first half hour of the day. He wore a dark scowl on his face. I never saw him smile and couldn't imagine him laughing. I understand now why he resented me so deeply, but can I just share with you men—holding your wife hostage through your bitterness will never be the solution to your marriage pain.

I am so thankful for the humble and grateful man that LeRoy has become. I encourage you to go to God, ask Him where you are on this issue. Confess to God your bitterness and resentment. Cry out to Him for grace to walk in humility and gratitude.

Grace: God's Empowering Response to Humility

I've been hitting you pretty hard (LeRoy again), but now we come to the sweet spot of walking with God. Now we come to the source of power for your battle. If you had a great marriage, with a kind, loving, and basically sinless wife, you would still need grace. Because you would still have at least one sinner who would require help. Thankfully, God's help is close at hand:

"Let us then with confidence draw near to the throne of grace, that we may receive mercy and find grace to help in time of need" (Hebrews 4:16).

If your marriage is anything close to how difficult ours was, you need a dump-truck load of grace! In marriage conferences, I often refer to marriage as a "grace factory." It's not that marriage necessarily produces grace, but it is grace at work and grace in constant motion. A difficult marriage is the grinding work of grace in our lives. The grinding of grace produces a beautiful masterpiece.

As you receive God's grace to cope with the day-to-day struggles, He grinds away at the burs of selfishness in your life. This allows God's grace to flow and move freely in your relationship. Small triumphs of grace will cause you to long for, and cry out for, more grace. Grace multiplies as you receive grace and extend grace. Grace extended becomes a trickle that soon becomes a downpour and then a flood of God's goodness.

The greatest opportunity in your life to experience the greatest work of God's grace will come about because of your greatest need. But beware, you can miss out and fall short of the grace and power that God has available to you (Galatians 5:4).

I want you to do a little mental exercise with me, or it might even be better to actually do this exercise by putting the book down and following these directions: Make a fist with your hand. Now, bend your arm where your fist is level with your chest, like you're holding a coffee cup at chest level. This is an exercise to show you what happens when you or I live in pride. That fist represents you.

Now, do the same thing with your other hand, make a fist and push that fist into the one you're already holding up—almost like they're "butting heads" with one another. This second fist represents God. This is the picture of what your life looks like when you are operating in pride. God is in opposition to you. You and He are pushing against each other in opposing directions. Read this verse carefully, then put your fists together in front of your chest so you can actually see what is happening if you've not humbled yourself before God:

"Clothe yourselves, all of you, with humility toward one another, for 'God opposes the proud but gives grace to the humble'" (1 Peter 5:5).

God opposes the proud. Let that truth sink in. You wonder why things are so hard. You wonder why your prayers aren't answered.

You wonder why your wife treats you with contempt. If you haven't humbled yourself, God is standing in opposition to you. Grace is needed, but you will not receive God's grace (His empowering work) without humility.

And the first step of humility is confession of your sin. As we've walked through this very tough chapter, have you experienced the ugly resistance of pride? Have you felt defensive? Maybe slammed the book shut a few times?

I know from experience that when you're feeling like a complete failure in your marriage—the last thing you want to hear is more of what you are doing wrong. But trust me, brother, I'm not here to slam you, I'm here to hold out a rope of rescue for you.

The day God broke me and showed me my fear of Kim was a deeply humbling work that ripped away my prideful façade that believed it was all her fault. God's grace to work in marriages is often blocked by a stronghold of sin in some area of our lives and pride prevents us from recognizing that sin. And in our pain, we justify our sin because we see our spouse's sin so clearly, that it blinds us to our own. But when God graciously opens our eyes, a window of escape is also opened. My window of escape was opened at a small guesthouse at a Texas ranch.

God had already been at work, working like a demolition ball, hitting at my pride and self-righteousness. He had been exposing all of that sinful ugly kind of garbage that we can hide so well most of the time. But when I got alone at that ranch house, just me and God, I no longer had anywhere to hide, no fig leaves to piece together, and no rocks to climb under. As God led my thoughts through a review of my life, He lovingly and clearly showed me that I was trapped in a prison of my own making. I realized I had a choice: receive God's grace by humbling myself through confessing my sin—or continue in my pride and remain trapped.

Fear was the stronghold, the prison, and I was held captive there. When He finally opened my eyes to my sinful fear, I did what, for years, I'd counseled others to do. I pulled open my Bible and read every verse or passage that related to that sin, in my case—sinful fear. Fear that blocked faith. Fear that choked out love. Fear that gave the enemy a place to work in my life. Fear that constricted worship and the work of God in my life. Every area of my life was twisted by fear . . . especially my role as the spiritual leader and husband to my wife.

My heart continued to soften as I agreed with God about my sinful condition. With each confession, pride was melting and God's grace was taking over. I began experiencing the healing power of grace.

For you, it may not be a capitulation to fear, but there is probably some stronghold that you've not yet allowed God to demolish. As we've walked through the last chapter, and now this one, has God opened your eyes to anything? Will you allow God's grace to work by humbling yourself?

HOW GRACE AFFECTS THE COURAGEOUS LEADER:

* He recognizes that grace is the great leveling factor—leaving no room for a superior attitude or a victim mentality.
* He keeps his gaze fixed on Christ; focusing on His position and character.
* He rests in the knowledge that God is sovereign and always at work; therefore he can trust Him to accomplish what is needed in his life.
* He cries out to Him for help rather than forging ahead in his own strength.
* As he learns to walk and respond consistently in grace, he is conformed to the image of Christ, and able to love his wife as Christ loves the Church.

Can you relate to any of what I'm sharing with you? I'm not pounding you with truth to beat you down and I certainly don't want to add to your pain by putting you on a guilt trip. But the reality is—your wife is not all the problem. You and I can enable our wives to live out their fierceness in a destructive manner, but we're called to protect them spiritually, and we can't come alongside and lead them out of their sin—unless we first deal with our own sin. Receiving, living in, and giving out God's grace is what will provide the transformation that you and your wife both need.

Humility opens the doorway for God to move in with grace that transforms, grace to overcome the temptation to sin, and grace that brings rich growth and maturity. The thing we most desperately need in our marriages is God's grace. *What I most desperately need in my life is God's grace.* When I acknowledge that need and cry out to God for grace (His empowering help for that specific situation), He pours it out in full measure and creative ways.

I encourage you to pray right now. Ask the Holy Spirit to reveal to you the one area in your life, or the one stronghold of sin, that is blocking God's grace from accomplishing God's will in your life at this time. You probably knew the answer before you finished reading the sentence. Bring your confession before the Lord with sincerity and a desperation to be right with Him.

Now, search the Scriptures for truth that applies specifically to your area of sin. Begin to commit to memory key passages. Humble yourself by sharing with your wife what God has shown you, how He has convicted you. Ask for her forgiveness. She may be shocked or she may show little reaction. Your wife may not initially respond, but the grace-blocking stronghold has been removed from your life.

God will begin to work. Get ready!

⊰ DIGGING IN ⊱

1. Luke 22 is a lengthy and graphic chapter. Within these seventy-one verses we find examples of each of the heart issues we've discussed: Fear, Ingratitude, and Pride. As you read, note when you recognize each of these and consider the outcome.

2. Study Jesus' interaction in prayer in the last hours before His arrest: Luke 22:39–46 and Matthew 26:36–46. What stands out to you in these accounts? How did Jesus respond to the mission that was before Him? What warnings did He give to His disciples?

3. What do you appreciate most about Jesus in these accounts? How can you apply His example to your situation?

What Your Wife Needs Most

That's written on your soul, brother, by God Almighty.
Big or little, strong or weak, night or day, you go up against
the enemy first. Woe to the husband—and woe to the nation—
that send their women to fight their battles.[1]

JOHN PIPER

We were seven years into our marriage when we took a family trip to Niagara Falls in a borrowed pop-up camper. It was late fall and we took our time exploring while stopping along the way at small campgrounds. We drove along the Canadian border and then dropped down into Michigan. We're from the South and when we first got a glimpse of this massive lake covered in snow, Kim started bouncing in her seat insisting that we stop and check it out.

Now, let me insert here, that as a man (as most husbands do), I take my responsibility of "protector" for my family seriously. However, it can be an extremely challenging task to attempt protection maneuvers with a headstrong, fierce wife in the mix. This strange mix has almost spelled disaster in our lives on more than one occasion. Maybe you can relate.

We found a roadside park with a view of (frozen) Lake Michigan, so I pulled into the deserted parking lot. Kim bounded out of the car and immediately ran toward the (frozen) beach while I unstrapped our three-year-old daughter from her car seat. From the shore, all we could see of the lake was white frozen waves (yes, frozen solid) covered in snow with huge chunks of ice in the distance. No sign of water, just a solid mass as far as the eye could see. I'm intentionally using the word frozen repeatedly because you need to get that picture thoroughly imbedded in your mind to appreciate my dilemma.

Kim insisted on walking out far enough to actually "see" Lake Michigan. Now, I need to mention again, we're from the South . . . we've never been around frozen bodies of water other than small ponds. We're taking a risk telling you this story, realizing that you could lose confidence in anything else we have to say, but at least you'll know we're being honest and transparent, I mean—who would publicly admit to what I'm about to share with you?

I'm the man. I'm duty-bound to serve my family as their "protector," and I had a really bad feeling that walking out onto a partially frozen mass the size of Lake Michigan was probably not a good idea. But my adventurous and ever-inquisitive wife had no fear. She was sure we could just cross a few yards of frozen waves and be able to get a good glimpse of the water with no problem at all. No amount of wise warnings or strong cautionary admonitions fazed her. She was determined to see that water and her insistence and giddy excitement made my appeals seem cowardly. She wouldn't take no for an answer and if

WE BEGAN THE UNWISE TREK ACROSS THE FROZEN PORTION OF THE LAKE WITH OUR TODDLER BETWEEN US, HOLDING HANDS TOGETHER.

you're married to a fierce woman, you know what I mean.

Kim's intensity squashed my instinct to protect. We began the unwise trek across the frozen portion of the lake with our toddler between us, the three of us holding hands together. Little did our daughter know how precarious her position was!

It never occurred to Kim the danger we were in as we started crossing the terrain of frozen waves. She just kept pressing forward to see the meeting point of ice and water. I had a bad feeling, and could hear the ice cracking and popping at points. I could not convince my fierce woman to turn back, but thankfully, someone with a badge stopped us before disaster sucked us under (literally).

We were probably a hundred yards out when we heard a loud bullhorn blare and megaphone-enhanced orders: "Turn around! Come back to your vehicle!" The police officer kept repeating his urgent instructions until he got our attention and we realized he was insisting for us to return to shore. The protector with the badge was able to do what I couldn't. Kim gave up her dream of seeing the lake's rolling waves and we started the long walk back to the beach.

The officer asked us what in the world we thought we were doing. Kim was quick to explain her plan to see the water. He looked at her like she was a complete idiot and asked her, "Where are you from?" When he realized that we were from a small town in the South, he was convinced that we were pitiful enough to let go, that we weren't intentionally endangering a minor (today they would've called child protective services), but mercifully, he didn't arrest us or take us to the loony bin.

Rules of Engagement

When we talk about that story now, both of us cringe and feel sick when we think about the danger. Today, Kim admits that she's amazed by how her fierce determination overcame her practical senses. But it wasn't the last time that happened. We've often clashed on what our course of action should be. She's the risk-taker; I'm the cautious one. But I'm also the one with the God-given role of "protector."

Now, let me state right up front that women are not in need of protection because they are frail or incapable. If you have a wife, God has entrusted you with a valuable treasure, and your willingness to guard that treasure from harm whether it be physical, spiritual, or emotional harm, is a demonstration of your love and commitment to her. Adam failed on this count. In chapter 3, we saw when Eve faced her greatest danger, he went passive on her. Adam did not serve Eve as her protector and we've been paying the consequences of that failure ever since.

Adam followed his wife's lead when she crossed the line to disobey God. Eve made the choice to consume the forbidden, but when it came time for God to confront the first couple for their disobedience, He didn't approach both of them together to hash it out. God called Adam to give an account because he had the responsibility of leadership and protection (Genesis 3:1–11). (Remember, He confronted Adam first before conversing with Eve?)

WOMEN CRAVE THE SECURITY THAT MALE PROTECTION WAS CREATED TO PROVIDE.

You don't need anyone to tell you that you should be a protector. You intuitively know. It is an integral part of being a husband, father, brother, patriot . . . a man. Within every man is the "Protection DNA." It can't be seen under a microscope, but it's there. It was placed there by our Creator and built into us with our assignment to provide and protect those who are entrusted to our care. Even though male leadership has come under attack, even though some women will bite your head off when you attempt to hold the door for them, women crave the security that male protection was created to provide. We regularly hear from women crying out for male protection and leadership. Your wife may not admit it, but that craving is in her DNA.

There is a seismic shift occurring that affects the most basic examples of guardianship. "To serve and protect" is a phrase that law enforcement agencies live by. But within the last few decades, the idea of serving and protecting has come under hostile scrutiny, as some no longer see law enforcement agencies as safe guardians of the public. In fact, the whole idea of "protection" seems often to be perceived as a threat rather than a heroic activity—at least when it comes to men or civil authorities.

Modern culture trashes the idea of male chivalry, twisting the idea of "male protection" into a warped male chauvinism and confusing the role of male protection by denigrating protective actions of manhood. When the cultural shift emasculated the American male, it stripped us of our protector status and many of today's men seem relieved to no longer carry that mantle.

During the months we were working on this book, US Defense Secretary Ashton Carter announced the decision to open all jobs in combat units to female members of the military. His announcement brought cheers from those celebrating this new "victory" for women's equality, while seasoned military leaders were disregarded when they sounded an alarm of warning. There are no longer clear lines delineating the role and character of a protector. And if you propose the idea that the role of husbands should be that of a "protector" you find that you're swimming hard upstream against the political correctness torrent.

Just Google "men protecting women" and you'll get several sources with a famous Susan B. Anthony quote: "I declare to you that woman must not depend upon the protection of man, but must be taught to protect herself, and there I take my stand." Her sentiments provide a concise summation of our culture's ideological shift.

Not only do we have the pressure of societal change, but there is the very real possibility that your wife fears placing herself in the position to be "protected." A large percentage of women we counsel have been abused by the male "protector"—whether it was a father figure or a teen boyfriend—and the harm caused by perversions of the protector role have produced a new generation of women who run from the suggestion that they need a "protector."

Before we were married, Kim shared with me how she was affected by being sexually molested as a child by a male figure she had once respected and viewed as someone she could trust to protect her. But it wasn't until many years into the marriage that Kim began to understand the connection between her fierce attitude toward men and the damage done by her perpetrator. She determined at a very young age that she'd never again allow a man to hold her down and harm her, either physically or emotionally. And so she became a fighter. Maybe your wife is as well.

Or yours may be a much different challenge. Perhaps your wife was well taken care of by a wise and loving father who she still holds in her heart as her primary protector, and you've never been able to step into that role because of a sense that you could never mea-

HOW DO HUSBANDS PROVIDE PROTECTION FOR A WIFE WHO SEEMS TO NEED NO PROTECTION?

———◆———

sure up to his hero status. He is older and more experienced than you, and seems to be an expert on all things, and unfortunately your "Charlie Brown" side always shows up whenever you're around him. Your wife may not even realize that she's still looking to her father as her real protector and comparing you as an inferior replacement.

If you're anything like me, you want to be your wife's champion. When danger threatens, you want to hold her close and assure her that you've "got this." You want to be her hero, protector, and knight in shining armor, all rolled into one. The rub comes when we husbands know that protecting our wives is our responsibility (and privilege), but our culture undermines our role and our wives reject our attempts to protect and serve them.

How do husbands—of strong, independent, self-protective wives—provide protection for a woman who seems to need no protection? In fact, for the first several years of our marriage, I felt like I was the one who needed to be protected from her! You may feel so inadequate as her "protector" that you've given up that idea long ago.

Don't lose heart . . . you were made for this battle. I have no doubt that you can fulfill the role that God created you to fill. Scripture points to Christ, our model, as a protector, so let's get some help by looking at Him.

God laid out His plan for mankind to know and understand Him by designing a living metaphor to convey His grand mystery. Marriage is to serve as a picture of the gospel. God's purpose in marriage is to use it as a physical picture to display to the world the beauty and holy character of His relationship with His bride, the church.

> Husbands, love your wives, as Christ loved the church and gave himself up for her, that he might sanctify her, having cleansed her by the washing of water with the word, so that he might present the church to himself in splendor, without spot or wrinkle or any such thing, that she might be holy and without blemish. In the same way husbands should love their wives as their own bodies. He who loves his wife loves himself. For no one ever hated his own flesh, but *nourishes* and *cherishes* it, just as Christ does the church, because we are members of his body. (Ephesians 5:25–30, emphasis mine)

In this passage, God provides us with insight into this mysterious work and gives us a clear pattern for functioning in our role as husband. The husband provides for and cherishes—protects. The

Greek term that is translated "cherishes" has the idea of tenderly "brooding over" to warm, giving the idea of a mother hen protecting her chicks from the cold. Jesus presented this idea when He told Jerusalem, "How often would I have gathered your children together as a hen gathers her brood under her wings, and you were not willing!" (Matthew 23:37)

Self-protection is a natural instinct. If you're cold, you'll grab a sweatshirt to warm up. If you know you're about to be hit, you'll instinctively move to protect your body. It is an involuntary reaction to potential harm and pain. The instinct to protect your wife should supersede your desire for self-protection.

Although Jesus did not take an earthly bride to protect, He provided us with a beautiful example of protecting His followers (who were the foundation of the church—the bride of Christ). John, an eyewitness in the garden, gives us the details. When a bloodthirsty mob came to arrest Jesus in the dead of night, rather than running, instead of using His disciples as a shield or letting them take up arms to defend Him, Jesus stepped forward and placed Himself between the disciples (members of His bride) and the danger (John 18:4). He stepped forward to protect, and stood in the gap to defend those He loved.

After stepping forward, Jesus took the initiative, not waiting for His hand to be forced but leading with authority. He asked, "Who are you looking for?" Unlike the first Adam, Jesus didn't remain silent in the face of danger but met the attackers head-on.

The angry mob witnessed one of the most fascinating displays of God's power, as the glory of God fell on them like a weapon knocking them down. A flash of God's manifest presence served not only as a holy stun gun to the enemies, but as a protective shield for His disciples when its force flattened the mob to the ground (John 18:6).

Jesus remained resolute as He continued to exert His authority and demonstrate leadership in protecting His friends. When we come to verse 8 there is no ambiguity about His concerns: they are for the ones He loved, not for Himself. He said, "Let these men go," boldly declaring His desire to take the full blow of the enemies' assault. Jesus knew His assignment and lived out every facet of His responsibility.

To end this account, John tells of Jesus protecting Peter and the other disciples from "themselves." Matthew adds that Jesus used this moment to teach the disciples lessons that would protect them in the future. As the protector, you must be ready to step in the gap between spiritual danger and your wife. She may want to jump in, unsheathe her sword, and swing it around wildly, but you are called to calmly control the situation with quiet confidence and strength. As you lead and protect her, you will have the opportunity to teach her important lessons as you grow in grace together.

I'm going to walk us through some practical ways that we can serve our wife as her protector. There is no "one-size-fits-all-super-hero" that I'm going to present to you, but Jesus gives us the clear example of how to lead in the most difficult circumstances. His lessons are clear, men. In the next five chapters, we'll use the word P-R-O-T-E-C-T-I-O-N as an acronym with "Action Points" that will help us to consider how to flesh out "laying down our lives" and loving our wife as Christ loves the Church in the role of her protector. And we begin with the letter "P."

P: PRAY LIKE A WARRIOR

In chapter 2, Kim shared how she told a marriage counselor that—more than anything else—she wanted me to pray with her. That floored me. I wasn't prepared for that response. I could pray with other people, I was a pastor, for crying out loud, but I was afraid to pray with my own wife. So, if you're struggling with that, I totally understand.

The first, and I believe most important, act of leadership as a husband is to pray (out loud) over your wife. Prayer is the most sacred and intimate act of worship that a husband and wife can experience together. It is an intertwining of the couple's hearts and souls with their God. Something powerful and unexplainable happens in the spiritual realm, and also in your wife's heart, when you pray together. The spiritual realm recognizes your authority when you take up your sword and shield as protector and defender, and pray for your wife.

It is a spiritual discipline and a glorious "assignment" from God—but it is also extremely hard to do when you're struggling just to survive. For years, I resisted having regular prayer times with my wife. I felt like Kim was more spiritual than I, prayed more than I, knew the Bible better than I . . . in every way I felt that she was superior to me, so what could I offer in the way of spiritual leadership? Who was I to pray over her? I didn't think that she needed me nor my help in any way. Now, I didn't voice these things, but deep down that was at the heart of my resistance.

Your wife may be much different than mine. She may not even want prayer, may not claim to believe in God. You still have the responsibility to serve as her spiritual leader. She needs you to be her spiritual prayer warrior no matter what. You are responsible to provide the spiritual safe haven for your wife. The disciples often showed Jesus that they didn't want to be led, would resist His intentional lessons and were dense to spiritual truths, but that didn't deter Jesus from fulfilling His responsibility to lead them spiritually. One of your most difficult challenges will be to protect your fierce woman from herself. God brought both of you together to complete His perfect work of sanctification—and that process occurs when you apply His truth and grace to your tumultuous union.

There are rich promises in 1 Peter for the man who seeks to

honor God and honor his wife, and we'll investigate that in the last
chapter, but right now, let me challenge you with some "Action
Steps." Start out your commitment to protect your wife through
prayer by asking God to provide you with the grace to be the man,
the spiritual leader in your relationship, and prayerfully walk
through these steps.

Action Steps:

Grab on to Grace First!

Spend some time in prayer, crying out for God's grace and help
to take leadership in the area of praying with your wife. Before
you approach her with the suggestion that the two of you begin
praying together, take advantage of the help offered in these
Scriptures: James 4:1–10; 5:16–18.

Confess and Seek Forgiveness

Tenderly but confidently talk with your wife and ask her forgiveness for failing to provide spiritual leadership in the past. She
may not react in a positive or forgiving way at first, so prepare
yourself for that. Don't enter in with any expectations, but do
this because it is the right thing to do.

Make the Commitment

Commit to pray for her in specific ways daily. If you go to bed at
different times (which I don't recommend), invite your wife to
pray with you before turning out the lights. Praying with her at
mealtimes is the perfect opportunity to pause together and be
thankful, and I hope you're doing that, but praying with her for
an extended period (it may only be two to three minutes at first)
about specific issues will minister needed grace to her. Pray specifically for obstacles she may face the next day, while expressing

to God your thankfulness for her and for the moments you spent together that day. Seek God's blessing on her life, and speak to God about her, your precious treasure. These moments will be an invaluable gift to your wife.

Don't Panic, Pray!

When your wife seems stressed, expresses fears or concerns, is emotional or having a meltdown . . . don't run, don't panic, don't shut down. This is the fire alarm sounding to let you know it is time to step up to the plate, take your wife gently by the hand, and offer to pray for her right then and there. Don't wait. It doesn't matter if you're in the mall or on the Interstate, pray immediately. Don't let fear or the emotional fireworks stop you. Pray with your wife! Calling on God's grace invites the Holy Spirit into the problem. I've been amazed by the power of the Spirit when I stop whatever I'm doing, take Kim's hand, and offer to pray with her about the stressful situation she is facing.

Keep Your Commitment!

Whatever you do, don't promise your wife that you will lead her spiritually and then back down from that commitment. If you miss a day, start over, but go into this process with the same determination that you would exert if your house was on fire and you needed to rescue your wife. Your house is on fire. Your wife does need your rescue. Kneeling to pray with your wife is her lifeline to safety!

Before we close this chapter, Kim wants to say a word to you about this . . .

When LeRoy first made the attempt to pray with me, it was with fear and trembling, but I was so grateful. Your wife may not yet realize how much she needs your prayers, but I promise you—this is a spiritual battle and you will see the impact on your wife. She needs you to serve her in this way and to fight for her as her prayer warrior.

As LeRoy began keeping his daily commitment to pray with me, my respect for him grew more than I could have ever imagined. That's been almost twenty years ago now, and

YOUR WIFE DOES NEED YOUR RESCUE. KNEELING TO PRAY WITH YOUR WIFE IS HER LIFELINE TO SAFETY!

he never misses a day. Ever. If we're in different cities, or across the globe from each other, he calls to pray with me. If he can't reach me, he leaves a voice mail with his prayer for me. I am eternally grateful that I live under the protection of my husband's prayers.

What about your wife—does she have your spiritual protection?

Okay men, I (LeRoy) know that at this point, you may be thinking, "There is NO way I could attempt those action points. There is no way I can do what you're asking me to do. You don't know my wife, you have no idea what she's like and what I'm up against."

She may be like the woman who sent this note to Kim:

> I personally related to where you said that other women observed that you intimidated men . . . I had been told that as well. To tell you how hard my heart had become, I had taken it as a compliment. I was raised in a very abusive family, and both parents were strong-willed and lived their entire life in rebellion to God.

Fierce women who take pride in intimidating the men in their lives—we see it all the time. In the face of such fierceness what is a man to do? How does a man marshal "marital manhood" in order that he might prevail as a protector for his wife?

I'll admit, learning to lead and protect a fierce woman takes a special man. It isn't easy and it doesn't happen overnight. It was almost two decades before I began to have hope.

Remember our walk on frozen Lake Michigan? You'd think my

fierce wife might have learned her lesson. After that, I had hopes that she would be more inclined to listen to my warnings. But only seven years later, on another family vacation to South Dakota—this time with two little ones in tow—Kim struck out on another adventure.

With plenty of clear warnings about the dangers of approaching the bison that roamed the area (plastered on signs and tourism literature), my fierce woman hopped out of the car and took off across the open fields to get closer to the herd so she could "just snap a few good pics." No number of warnings slowed her down one bit. She ignored the signs, she ignored me, but when she heard the park ranger's bullhorn blasting in the distance (yes, another civil servant had to stop her) with instructions to "Get back in your VEHICLE!!" she complied.

Yep, gentlemen, I've got one strong woman on my hands.

How do you protect a woman who thinks she needs no protection?

How do you lead a headstrong female like that?

The answer is clear. And in the next chapter, we're going to share with you the most crucial aspect that is needed in order for you to have the power (and desire) to lead your fierce woman well. Just a note of warning: put on some heavy-duty running shoes and get ready for a marathon!

⊰ Digging In ⊱

1. In this chapter, we witnessed Jesus protecting His disciples when the mob came to arrest Him. Just before this, Jesus had prayed for His followers (including you and me). Read through that prayer in John 17 and watch for patterns in His prayer that indicate His commitment to serving His bride as her "Protector." How can you apply this example as you pray for your wife?

2. One of the primary responsibilities of the husband is seen in Christ's example of cleansing His bride by washing her in the Word (Ephesians 5:26). He reiterates this cleansing property of the Word in His prayer (John 17:17). How are you protecting your bride by washing her in the Word? How can you be intentional in serving her in this way?

God's Got This!

Battles are won, not with weapons, but with God.
They are won where the way leads to the cross.[1]

DIETRICH BONHOEFFER

The movie hadn't started yet. Previews of new releases were running, so there was still enough low lighting to get a good view of the brawl breaking out down front. Two young men were pushing and shoving each other and it looked like the early signs of a fight. Just as things were getting heated, a middle-aged woman came running down the center aisle toward the scuffle. She tried to insert herself as a barrier between the two, but one of the men held out his arm to try and keep her at a distance. My son, who was relaying this story to me, said the entire theatre heard the young man turn to the woman he was pushing away (as he was being punched by the other man) and yell at her, "Mom! I've got this!" The audience burst into laughter.

Sounds like that young man was raised by one fierce momma. She was still trying to serve as his protector! We introduced the P-R-O-T-E-C-T-I-O-N acronym in the last chapter and gave you some "Action Steps" to start fleshing out the content we're sharing. How is that going?

Let me give you a friendly—but man to man—charge: if you're just skimming this book and not applying the truth we're sharing, you're really not interested in change, or it could be that you've reached such a low point—that you've lost all hope for change, and your energy is zapped. I was there. I know how hard it is to put forth effort when it seems like every attempt to move forward knocks you further back. If that's where you are, hang in here a bit longer because this chapter is critical and holds the key to transformation.

And for the man who may be reading, but isn't applying himself to change because he thinks his wife is all the problem, or you're convinced "I've got this!" let me just say (in love)—you don't have this. If that's your attitude, you don't have a clue. In order to protect your wife, it will require one thing, and this is the most important and necessary ingredient, and what your wife desperately needs for you to do: run to the cross!

How do you bridge the chasm between who you know God has created you to be and who you are most days? How do you live out the example of Christ and love your wife the way He's called you to love her? How do you provide leadership and protection for a woman who seems superior to you in every way?

The first step to bridge that chasm begins with running to the cross.

R: RUN TO THE CROSS

Running a little more than twenty-six miles to complete a grueling marathon takes physical endurance but also mental toughness. The runner must discipline himself mentally in those last miles of the race; when his lungs are burning and his legs are wobbling, his focus must be on the finish line.

The writer of Hebrews provides the solution for the man who is weary and fainthearted in life's race. He charges us to lift up our drooping hands and strengthen our weak knees, but most importantly, he tells us where to fix our eyes—on the cross:

> . . . let us run with endurance the race that is set before us, looking to Jesus, the founder and perfecter of our faith, who for the joy that was set before him endured the cross, despising the shame, and is seated at the right hand of the throne of God (Hebrews 12:1–2).

If we could actually be present at Jesus' crucifixion, the horror of the cross would cause us to want to run from the brutality, or at least drop our eyes. This cruel form of capital punishment was the form of death that the Father chose for His Son as He placed our sins on Him.

Jesus Christ endured the righteous wrath of God, poured out on His beaten and bleeding body, in order to pay the price to redeem mankind from the wages of sin—death. Remember that forbidden fruit that the first couple was so quick to eat? That act of treason birthed our death (Romans 3:23–25; 5:12–15). You, me, all of us are under the curse of a death sentence. We are born spiritually dead. Our only hope for eternal life after physical death, and our only hope of abundant life now, is through the work that Jesus did for us on the cross. The cross is a cruel instrument of death, but at the same time, the cross is your only real hope.

At the cross, captives are liberated; prisoners are set free. Unless you come to God, through the work that Jesus did on the cross, you will always be a prisoner to your failures and held captive by your sinful addictions. Your only hope is the grace-work Jesus accomplished on the cross. And before we go any further, Kim and I want you to understand that.

When we sit down to counsel with a couple, we never assume that they understand the work of the cross, or that they have a relationship with Christ. They may be church members, may claim to be Christians—but mental assent to Christianity or social affiliation with a church is not the same as gospel transformation.

So, if you already have a relationship with Christ, as you walk through this next section let it serve as an opportunity for you to express your gratitude for what He's done for you. If you've never experienced what we're describing, then we ask you to be open to the work God desires to do in your life!

The first truth that all of us must understand and acknowledge, is that we cannot please God (that's you and me—all of us!) without God bringing about the change that is needed. In my natural state, I'm actually a rebel. In reality, I'm God's enemy. (This would be a good point to pause and read Ephesians chapter two.) But when I approach God, acknowledging my sin—confessing that I deserve the wrath of a Holy God, and with that confession, seek His forgiveness—then I can experience what I John 1:9 (NASB) declares:

"If we confess our sins, He is faithful and righteous to forgive us our sins and to cleanse us from all unrighteousness."

When you read the word "unrighteousness" think of crawling through a mud hole. You know, getting really filthy. What I mean by this kind of "filthy" is a spiritual and moral condition. So, think of the most rotten thing you've ever done and multiply that by the millions of other rotten things you've done—and not even considered as rotten in your life. That's the filthiness that Jesus placed on Himself. And it's not just your filthiness; it's the filth of the rebellious saints of all the ages that He took on. It is incredible to imagine the weight of that sin and corruption pressing down on the sinless Savior.

When I'm really filthy, all I can think of is getting a good, hot bath. Jesus wants to clean us up. That's you and me. He came to rescue us from our worst state (and even our "best" state). He came so that we don't have to stay in that filthy condition. He came to not only clean us up; He came to make us completely new (1 John 4:9–10; 2 Corinthians 5:17–21). Jesus exchanges His sinless state for our filthy condition. Amazing grace. Period.

Jesus came to do this. He is the Redeeming God. But redemption also has a broader aspect than just our salvation or "rescue" from eternal damnation (as huge as that is!); once you enter into a relationship with God, He begins His restoration process. He begins the grace operation! And grace is what a "loser" needs most.

One of the most difficult things about being married to a fierce woman is the feeling of worthlessness that can develop. No matter how hard you try to do the right thing, to please her, to be the fearless leader—somehow you always end up feeling like a loser. No matter how much you attempt to be the hero, Charlie Brown takes over. This is the point at which you need to learn how to "run to the cross."

When we realize that our "self-esteem," our worth and value, is found in what Christ did for us on the cross, we'll be secure. When we are solidly planted in God's love for us, when we are looking to Him alone as the One we are living to please, we will be oblivious to what others (including our wife) think of us . . . we will only care what He thinks of us.

> ONE OF THE MOST DIFFICULT THINGS ABOUT BEING MARRIED TO A FIERCE WOMAN IS THE FEELING OF WORTHLESSNESS THAT CAN DEVELOP.

When we are centering our lives and identity around the truth that we are valuable to God, when our personal esteem flows from His purchase of us through His shed blood, then we will be so caught up in that gracious reality that no matter what our wives do, they won't be defining our value—Christ will!

Getting Real Help

"Fierce women" often leave comments on Kim's website. If you think that your wife can never change, be encouraged by reading a couple of notes left by women who are undergoing God's "grace operation":

> I had been a very demeaning wife. Even kicking my husband in the shin one time while he was leading a Bible study because I thought he was saying the wrong thing! God has been so merciful to us and has restored our marriage and done more than we could hope for. Praise the Lord! He has used you . . . (as) a rare and much needed voice in the church today.

> Since I read *Fierce Women* and began living in the truth I found in Scripture, the response of my husband is nothing short of miraculous. His behavior and communication shows how a good man was hiding just outside the shadow of my wildly fierce presence in our marriage.

> I have been a very sad and fearful woman for a very long time. Now, my heart is overflowing with gratitude. Of course, I've had momentary lapses into wildness . . . but my husband, for the first time in all our married life, has actually moved to restore the relationship. When I look into his eyes, I see forgiveness where I saw contempt, confusion and callousness before. My husband is eager to move in victory over his passivity/fearfulness. He must believe that he now stands a chance!

Be encouraged knowing that God is aware of all you are facing. He provides grace and power for transformation—for both you and your wife. And He has provided a "Helper" for you to rely on in this process.

The work that Jesus did on the cross was necessary to rescue us from the penalty of sin. But that's not all—there is another exciting and personal aspect to having a personal relationship with God. Shortly before Jesus' death, as He was preparing the disciples for His departure from earth, He gave them this promise:

But I tell you the truth, it is to your advantage that I go away; for if I do not go away, the Helper will not come to you; but if I go, I will send Him to you. And He, when He comes, will convict the world concerning sin and righteousness and judgment . . . when He, the Spirit of truth, comes, He will guide you into all the truth . . . (John 16:7–13 NASB).

This "Helper" who Jesus mentions is God's Spirit. Once we've confessed our sin to God, asked for and received His forgiveness, the Holy Spirit then "takes up residence" in our soul, He "fills us" (Romans 8:9–11). Talk about having a personal relationship with God—when the Holy Spirit is living within us—THAT is PERSONAL!

Mankind was created in the image of God, with the purpose of reflecting God's worth and value (His glory), but sin marred man's holy, pure state. Man "fell short of the glory of God" when he rebelled. God's restorative work (sanctification) is designed to display the power of the gospel through transforming fallen men and women (this includes you and me!) into individuals whose lives bring glory to God. Sanctification occurs as we submit to the authority of God's Word, and apply His truth to our lives, through the grace and power of His Holy Spirit.

The Grace Operation at Work

Did you read that last statement? Change comes through the grace and power of the Holy Spirit—not by our puny efforts. Not by staying in my cave of safety! Not by telling God, "I've got this!" We don't have this. We need the Helper. We need the grace and power of the Holy Spirit to bring lasting change. That's the grace operation at work!

Brad reached out to us when his world was falling apart. His wife kicked him out of the house and was filing for divorce. Their marriage had been rocky from the start. He'd hidden his porn addiction for years, but one day she found out. She forgave him repeatedly and each time he promised it would be the last. But this time, Deb was done.

The threat of divorce was a wake-up call for Brad. He knew he'd betrayed his wife, betrayed God, and knew he deserved her wrath. But God was merciful and gracious. God plunged Brad into the grace operation. He started a work of restoration in Brad's heart and mind as Brad took action and ran to the cross. He confessed his sin to his wife, to his church leadership, and to men who became accountability partners.

Not only did God bring restoration to their marriage, but God has done a powerful and redeeming work in Brad's life. He is not the same man that his wife threatened to divorce. Running to the cross, on a daily basis, has brought lasting change to Brad, and all who know him recognize the power of the gospel to bring that change.

The exciting truth is this: God is able to take the difficulties of our lives, the struggles and also the blessings, and use them in the process of "growing us up" and conforming us to the image of Christ. When we enter into a relationship with God and learn to cry out to Him for help to apply the truth of His Word to the critical need of the moment—God will not fail us. His Word does not fail us. "God's got this" is the accurate way to view the problem of leading your fierce wife.

Before God opened my eyes to this, I was attempting to be a good husband to Kim and I took it personally whenever she seemed disappointed with my efforts. Things took on a completely different mode of operation and outcome when I began looking to Christ, asking Him for grace, power, and wisdom from the Holy Spirit, to function in moments of failure and need.

Before Jesus offered Himself in our place on the cross, mankind's relationship with God was dependent on his best efforts. Adam tried to fix things with fig leaves (Genesis 3:7), but our best efforts, our attempts to "work our way to God," will never bring deliverance from sin and the transforming work of grace that we so desperately need. The cross provides the grace you need for salvation and the grace you need to lead your fierce woman.

The gospel (good news) is this: Jesus Christ was sinless but "became sin" in order to pay our sin debt. He died and was buried, but through the power of God, He rose to life. That same resurrection power is available to those who come to God, asking forgiveness for their sins, and receiving the work of grace that Jesus performed on the cross. The power that God provides because of the cross is the power you need for your salvation, for your personal spiritual growth, for abundant living. It is the power you need to lead your fierce woman.

Without the gospel, attempting to employ these practical changes and establish new habits in your relationship with your wife is nothing more than behavior modification. In order to see true, resurrection-power transformation, we must run to the cross. God is able to use what you are walking through today, in this moment, to fulfill the purpose He created you for! Let that give you hope. Let truth sustain you in the last miles of the race!

Action Steps:

Admit Your Need

Admit to God that you don't have this—you need Him. If you've never humbled yourself before God, admitting that you're a sinner in need of a Savior, spend some time in Ephesians chapter two and grapple with the reality that you need to be rescued from your sinful condition. You can cry out to Him for salvation while you're completely alone. Or you might consider asking a pastor or spiritual leader that you respect to walk with you through this process. The road to real peace and victory in your life begins here. There is no hope for your future without going to the cross first.

Adopt the Cross as Your Default Position

When you're frustrated, angry, hurt, or tempted to indulge in sinful addictions—let the cross become your go-to place for daily rescue. Begin to adopt the regular process of "crying out." Spend some time reading through the book of James and follow the example we see in chapter four of humbling ourselves before God, drawing near to Him, and receiving His help in time of need.

Stand Naked

Let the cross strip you of your "victim mentality." Go to the cross and recognize that Jesus was stripped naked as your substitute. He allowed Himself to be placed under public scrutiny and degradation—in your place! When you consider what He's done for you, you have no platform for holding on to "victimhood." You've been stripped of that. He willingly hung as a victim of man's cruelty and injustice in your place. You are no longer a victim when you recognize the grace and mercy you've been given at the cross. Let the cross strip you naked from the façade of "victim."

Grow in the Fruit of the Spirit

As you develop the "default position" of running to the cross, the fruit of the Spirit will begin to show up in your life in increasing measure: love, joy, peace, patience, kindness, goodness, faithfulness, gentleness, and self-control (Galatians 5:16–26). This is not a "behavior checklist" but will become an overflow of the grace-work in your life.

At the cross, the work of "making all things new" is complete.

Because of the cross, your new way of living, new desires, and new victories are a credible reality. The death at the cross holds within it the promise of the resurrection.

As we continue working our way through the P-R-O-T-E-C-T-I-O-N acronym, keep in mind that each of the topics and "Action Steps" that we address are only possible when you run to the cross. This is not a "self-help" manual, but it is a "grace-operation manual" empowered by the grace-work of the cross.

O: OPEN YOUR MOUTH

One of the most difficult things that the husband of a fierce woman can do is—talk to her! I mean, engaging in real heartfelt, getting-to-the-root-of-the-problem communication. I know what you're thinking right now. "You've got to be kidding me, you don't know my wife! She talks, I listen. End of story. Talk to her? I can't. I'm completely shut down. And if I attempt communication, it always ends up coming back to bite me. She'll use it against me." Or whatever excuses are filling your head right now . . . you fill in the blank. And so she talks and you shut down. She is hurt because you don't communicate. You're emasculated and resent her for it. And the wall between you grows higher.

WHAT IS THE FIRST STEP TO TEARING DOWN THAT WALL BETWEEN THE TWO OF YOU? OPEN YOUR MOUTH.

If this cycle is going to be broken, if this wall is going to be torn down, at some point you must step up to the plate—and open your mouth!

If you ever played Little League baseball, you know the pressure, the weakness in your knees, the churning in your belly. You remember? It seemed like every time it was your turn to bat, there would be at least two runners on base and two outs. All the pressure was on you. All eyes on you. Your teammates, coach, the other team, all twenty-three people sitting in the dilapidated bleachers, and your screaming mother shouting, "You can do it, son! Hit a home run!"

A home run? Good grief.

Silently, you prayed for four balls and the ump to yell, "Take your base!" You failed so many times before, but once again, you had to step up to the plate.

What is the first step to tearing down that wall between the two of you? Open your mouth. Make this a priority. You need to make sure that there will be no interruptions. Nothing pressing. Leave the phones in another room. Yes, seriously—leave the phones in another room! Start by gently but firmly letting her know that you have something to say. And ask her to please allow you to speak until you are finished. Begin by leading her in prayer. (Don't pray that she'll be changed, or that this will "fix" your marriage, or anything along those lines.) Ask God for help to say what is on your heart. Pray for His guidance and wisdom, and thank God for your wife as you pray.

Explain what God has been doing in your heart and what He's been showing you . . . where you've come up short in relation to His standards. This will be difficult. It will be humbling. But if you spent some time in the book of James (Action Step in last section), you know that humbling yourself is an integral part of the process of God working in your life, and it is necessary in order to receive God's grace.

Be open with your wife about your sins, shortcomings, and past failures. Don't justify or excuse your behavior. Express your love for her, but more importantly, your love for God and your trust in His Word. Let her know that you desire for your relationship to reflect God's design for marriage and in so doing, bring Him glory. Apologize for not leading her and loving her as Christ modeled. Restate your love, thankfulness, and appreciation for her. Renew your commitment to honor, cherish, and be faithful to her.

Don't expect her to immediately be ravishingly in love with you again. Don't expect her to respond in any particular way, in fact—don't place any expectations on her, but leave all of that to God. Let God be in control. After all, He is Almighty God. The important thing is that you've "opened your mouth" . . . broken Adam's silence and passivity. If you've done what God desired, your first step is completed.

As you grow in this process, you will learn that you lead by serving. You and I do not know what our wives need most of the time. They are confusing and complicated creatures, but God created them. Ask Him how you can live with your wife "in an understanding way" (1 Peter 3:7). Ask her some questions that will guide you to understanding her better (to do this, you'll be required to open your mouth again). Ask her, "What can I do to help you? How may I pray for you today?"

Many women battle insecurity and seem to interpret silence from their husband as a need to spring into action and take charge. Just a small increase in initiative (expressed verbally) will go a long way in calming her inner battle with insecurity and the urge to take charge. If your wife typically grabs all the speaking room and never gives the floor to you, it is time to let her know that you need "room to speak" so she can receive input from you. If you attempt to communicate that message and she totally rejects you, run to the cross again, and then reiterate the message with tender firmness. She needs that message from you. She needs your input and communication. The wall between you will never come down without it.

Action Steps:

Plan to Speak

Put a plan of action in place for this first "communication date." Get a babysitter if you have children in the home, block out a space of time free from interruptions, put the phones in another room (just do it!), and gently but courageously lead your wife through this honest conversation. Prepare yourself to "run to the cross" several times during this conversation.

Listen Well

Let your wife know that you want to learn how to really "hear" her and explain that sometimes that means that she'll need to give space in the conversation for you to move slowly in this process: asking questions as well as getting clarification from her. If it is difficult for you to really hear and understand her when a barrage of communication is hitting you, let her know it is like attempting to get a drink from a fire hydrant and you'd prefer sipping slowly from a glass.

Develop a New Communication Pattern

Have an honest discussion about what your communication pattern looks like now (who leads, who retreats, who dominates, who is passive) and dream together about a communication pattern that would be more enjoyable and helpful for both of you. If one of you is prone to interrupt the other, agree on a plan of action to alert the other partner to that issue (in a non-offensive way). Discuss how to develop the plan and schedule blocks of time for regular communication. If your wife is one who likes late night discussions and you have an early morning schedule, come up with a compromise that will provide an optimal time (as much as possible, anyway) and agree to try to hold off on heavy discussions until the time that you've already agreed is best.

HALT

In *Fierce Women*, I (Kim) gave the readers some advice, using the "HALT" acronym (which is not original with me, by the way). This may be more applicable to wives than husbands, but it's a good idea to discuss this principle together as you work on your new communication pattern. This isn't for "sweeping things under the rug" or avoiding difficult conversations, but you can use it as a protective device for times when it might be best to delay a conversation that has heavy content, or the potential for conflict and emotional meltdowns.

Here's how it works in relation to the tongue. Restrain your words (or more bluntly—shut your mouth) and delay weighty conversations when you are:

H — Hungry
A — Angry
L — Lonely
T — Tired

From a wife's perspective, let me assure you, if you sit down with your wife, give her your undivided attention, and let her know that you want to work on improving your communication as a couple—you will be her hero! She will be excited that you are taking the lead on tearing down that wall! Think of communication as a basic form of protection for your wife. As you clearly articulate your love and concern for her, it allays her fears. As you engage in the conversation (rather than remaining silent), you demonstrate your care and willingness to connect with her. Clear communication puts you both on the same page and that protects you from unnecessary misunderstandings.

Men, I (LeRoy) encourage you to begin applying what I'm sharing with you, not with the primary motive of winning your wife's heart—but out of love for your Savior. Focus on getting that relationship in line first, before moving on to work on your marriage relationship. There is no substitute for your personal walk with God.

> THINK OF COMMUNICATION AS A BASIC FORM OF PROTECTION FOR YOUR WIFE. AS YOU CLEARLY ARTICULATE YOUR LOVE AND CONCERN FOR HER, IT ALLAYS HER FEARS.

Regardless of your past failures, you must take ownership of the role of protector. Make it your mission and your life's work. Take personally the challenge to not lose your wife and your marriage. My weakness was "my weakness." I was weak because I was not surrendered fully to God. I was still depending on myself to be the husband that I knew I should be—but couldn't. God is not weak. His power is not puny. As you run to the cross and open your mouth to communicate, I pray that the resurrection power of our Savior will infuse you with fresh zeal and energy to be the man of God He's created you to be!

God's got this!

⊰ DIGGING IN ⊱

1. Running to the cross will provide you with the right perspective for dealing with the difficulties of marriage to a fierce woman. The cross defines your worth and value. Read Ephesians chapter one and take note of who you are "in Christ."

2. What are your instructions in Ephesians 5:1–2? How do you need to apply that in your relationship with your wife?

3. With those instructions as your basis for action, consider how to apply Ephesians 4:29–32 in the way you communicate with your wife.

CHAPTER 8

How She Wants You to Love Her

❖

Only if God's love is the most important thing to you
will you have the freedom to love your spouse well.[1]

TIMOTHY KELLER

The snow was blinding and we counted more than forty
vehicles in the ditch on our six-hour journey through
the Ouachita Mountains. We'd traveled to Northwest
Arkansas on Christmas Eve, and our plan was to spend Christmas
with LeRoy's family, but by Christmas morning the news was fore-
casting an unprecedented winter storm. The snow of the "2012
Christmas blizzard" piled up almost a foot, most of it falling within
a three-hour period—the three-hour period in the middle of our
six-hour journey through the mountain passes! We left his parents'
house early on Christmas Day, trying to get ahead of the storm and
make it home before dark. But about an hour into the drive, the
storm caught up with us and pummeled us all the way home!

I wasn't afraid though; I've been with LeRoy in worse storms and have confidence in his abilities to navigate and lead us through any blizzard. But early in our marriage, I didn't do so well accepting LeRoy's leadership. I was a headstrong young woman and I was not a good follower—at least when it came to following LeRoy's decisions. I think some of it had to do with the fact that he was so different from my father (and from me). My father could assess a situation quickly, determine the right course of action, and go into execute mode without hesitation. LeRoy's process is slow, sure, and methodical. Also, my father had several years of life experience under his belt and that put LeRoy in a rookie category.

In those days, we had conflicts regularly. We saw things differently, and I felt like LeRoy wasn't appreciating my input, wasn't even open to it, and the more distance he put between us during the decision-making process—the more I demanded to be involved and heard. I wasn't intending to strip him of leadership; I just wanted him to value my contribution. I didn't realize that my "input" was putting pressure on him to act when he was still in the early stages of deliberation.

Typically, I took his slow process as indecisiveness and would jump in to "fix" the problem or find a solution—not even realizing that by doing that I was robbing him of the opportunity to lead. When that became a pattern, he eventually handed over leadership to me. We claimed to be complementarians (theologically) but were functioning as egalitarians (practically).[2]

Some men "lead" through harsh domination (which isn't really leadership). They bulldoze their way through and set their agenda with no regard for anyone else. They don't lead, they just function as a controlling bully. Woe to the man who tries that with a fierce woman. He is just asking for an explosion!

Thankfully, LeRoy took the tender route in leadership. He eventually realized the need to explain to me his philosophy and process for making decisions, and sat down with me one day to explain the difference in his leadership style. He told me why he was slow and careful in his deliberations, and why "risk taking" was outside of his framework. That helped me to understand that he didn't intend to frustrate me with his slower pace, or that his quiet response didn't mean that he was ignoring the problem.

When he took the initiative and really began leading me spiritually, that provided me with the security to allow him to lead me in other areas. As I released control and began to look to him for leadership, he eagerly invited me into the decision-making process. We are a team. He values my input and I value his leadership. I am so grateful for the incredible changes we've seen in this area of our marriage, changes that God desires to bring to your marriage as well. We're continuing with the P-R-O-T-E-C-T-I-O-N acronym and have reached a critical component to your role as your wife's protector.

T: TENDERLY LEAD

Many of us have heard the old adage, "The way to a man's heart is through his stomach." Let me (LeRoy) suggest that the way to a woman's heart is through her soul. This means it can't be done in the flesh . . . depending on your best intentions or efforts. Peter's admonition to husbands (1 Peter 3:7) is an appeal to lead the wife's heart through serving her. Paul also charges men (in his letters to the churches in Ephesus and Colossae): "Husbands, love your wives."

To the Colossian husband he adds, "and do not be embittered them" (3:19 NASB). Why the statement about bitterness? Could it be that husbands (especially, Christian husbands) are more susceptible to the spiritual poison of bitterness—specifically in our relationship with our wife? Especially when she doesn't respect or affirm us?

After all, you are a follower of Jesus, you're trying to live right, and she still balks at following your leadership. Perhaps you begin to believe that you're being mistreated and the desire to love your wife through tender leadership—slowly dies.

You were destined to lead your wife spiritually. It is God's design. When God laid out His plan for marriage to serve as a visible demonstration of the gospel, He gave husbands the role of leadership. Commitment, self-sacrifice, and loving devotion characterize Christ's leadership of His bride—and it should characterize your leadership as well.

She may not even realize it, but deep down, your wife needs for you to lead her. But your leadership must flow out of your love relationship with Christ. As you humbly surrender to His lordship, that surrender provides the basis for your leadership—a leadership that must be Christlike, servant leadership, "as Christ loved the church and gave Himself for it" type of leadership. Leading your wife's heart comes from a total dependence and surrender of your heart to the Savior.

Right now some of you may be thinking, "I'm saved, I try to be a good husband. I've prayed. I've done everything I know how to do . . ." Brother, I've been right where you are and had those same thoughts. You know the problem with all of those statements? Too much "I" and not enough Jesus. Just sayin'.

God is no respecter of persons. If He changed me, He can change you. If He transformed our marriage, He can do it for your marriage, for His glory. God will always provide the grace to accomplish His will . . . always. What does a husband (who is a spiritual leader) look like?

When people tell me that I "don't look like a pastor," I always take that as a compliment (whether it's meant that way or not). Maybe it's my boots and Wranglers, or maybe I don't speak with a "preacher voice." It could be that I drive a 1975 three-quarter-ton four-wheel-drive pickup that I call "Ol' Red." Truth is, I'm not what people expect a pastor to "look" like, but I hope I live like what a husband is supposed to look like.

Do you know what God expects a husband to look like?

God makes a statement that answers that question. Every husband should sit up straight and take notice of this passage:

Thus says the Lord, "Let not a wise man boast of his wisdom, and let not the mighty man boast of his might, let not a rich man boast of his riches; but let him who boasts boast of this, that he understands and knows Me, that I am the Lord who exercises lovingkindness, justice and righteousness on earth; for I delight in these things," declares the Lord. (Jeremiah 9:23–24 NASB)

Did you notice the three characteristics that God delights in?

- Lovingkindness
- Justice
- Righteousness

> LOVINGKINDNESS IS THE OLD TESTAMENT EQUIVALENT OF THE NEW TESTAMENT WORD "GRACE." IT IS LOVE IN ACTION. LOVE ON DISPLAY. LOVE WITH WORK-BOOTS ON.

Do you think that if God delights in these traits of godliness that a Christian wife would probably delight in them as well?

The first one that He lists is: *lovingkindness.* Now, don't freak out on me. Demonstrating lovingkindness doesn't mean that you'll suddenly have to turn into some mushy, chick-flick-watching sap of a guy who is in danger of having his "man card" taken away. Don't shut down on me, just listen.

Lovingkindness is the Old Testament equivalent of the New Testament word "grace." It is love in action. Love on display. Love with work-boots on. It is far beyond temporary emotion or tentative commitment. This love is a kind, tenderhearted tough-as-nails love that weathers the worst of life's storms. This love is a rock-ribbed, rock-solid commitment that remains. When all else might be swept away, this type of bedrock love will remain. Lovingkindness, the love that reflects God's love, cannot be produced by mere human flesh—but it flows from a heart that responds to God's love by loving Him back and therefore is able to love and lead others.

The next characteristic that God takes pleasure in is: *justice*. You might be wondering, "What does 'justice' have to do with leading my fierce woman?" Hang with me, God has more to say about this.

Justice is a transferrable attribute of God (unlike omniscience or omnipresence). God is "just" and as we grow in Him, we will take on that trait as well. This part of God's character and who God wants us to become is developed by acting on God's wisdom: it is the judicious exercise of moral authority. Justice speaks of judgment, discernment, and decision making that aligns with God's Word. When God's truth captivates our wills and intellects, justice will preside over our decisions and actions. Good leadership requires functioning with justice.

As Christian men, day-by-day and moment-by-moment, we are to live out God's justice by our actions, our treatment of others, and our decision making. What does God require of us? "He has told you, O man, what is good; and what does the Lord require of you but to do justice, and to love kindness, and to walk humbly with your God?" (Micah 6:8).

The last of the three characteristics found in our Jeremiah passage is: *righteousness*.

Righteousness is the quality of a life that consistently chooses God's will and constantly places others' best interest above its own. Righteousness is "doing right" because your heart is right. It is the "working out" of your salvation (Philippians 2:12) through grace-empowerment. It is God's goodness flowing through a willing and clean vessel. It is certainly trusting God's righteousness (you and I have none without receiving His), but it is also taking a serious approach to living a holy life. The result of a righteous life will be a life that not only pleases God but also repels the darkness. Overcoming evil with good (Romans 12:21)—that's righteousness.

Jesus emphasized the call to this type of life in Luke 10:27. He told the young lawyer (and us) to "love the Lord your God with all your heart and with all your soul" (that's lovingkindness in action) "and with all your strength" (that's righteousness—holy life in action) "and with all your mind" (justice—the judicious exercise of moral authority and wisdom). This summation of the commandments is practically a restatement of Jeremiah 9:23–24.

Lovingkindness is the heart from which leadership should flow. Justice is the proper framework from which leadership can provide a template for wise decisions. Righteousness is the motivation for leadership: making leadership decisions on the basis of what is best for others and what will ultimately glorify God. All of these leadership characteristics are fleshed out through the greatest commandment: love God with all your heart, soul, strength, and mind, and love others out of the overflow of your love for God.

The point is, men, when our lives begin to reflect this level of Christlikeness, our wives will be more inclined to entrust themselves to our leadership. Our godliness is to be an unspoken shield of glory to protect and defend our wives. The qualities and characteristics of Christ are imminently more appealing and attractive than your best qualities or characteristics could ever be (even on your very best day)! As your wife begins to see Jesus in you, her heart is more likely to soften and her love and respect grow. You need Jesus. She needs Jesus. She needs to see Jesus in you. You need to show Jesus to her. This is at the core of transformational change. Change is only possible when it comes from the One who never changes.

As you begin to operate under the wisdom of the Word, and your servant-hearted devotion becomes apparent, you will have a platform to lead your wife. When she has the assurance that you've prayed through a decision, humbly listened to her input, sought the Word, and inclined your heart to be led by the Spirit, she will see in you the qualities of a tender leader and be more inclined to follow.

Action Steps:

Go Public

Let your wife know your plan of action. This is not a covert operation. If you are going to lead, she is going to know it. Ask her to pray for you. Let her know that you will probably fail at points and that you're depending on God's grace in executing this plan. Thank her in advance for her patience. Note: if your wife has zero interest in the leadership change, this process may have to "fly under the radar" for a bit. By that, I mean that you will need to depend on God to create opportunities for you to lead your wife when she's not really wanting your leadership. When those opportunities arise, you must be prepared to rise to the challenge.

Get Input

Look for an elderly (spiritually mature) believer that has an obviously healthy marriage and ask him to meet for coffee. Ask for specific ways that he's led his wife and how he's earned her love and respect.

Take a Daily Leadership Course

Did you know that there is a free leadership course available to you? If you commit to a daily discipline of reading a chapter per day from one of the Gospels, you'll find that it's an excellent resource manual—right at your fingertips! Read and ask God to teach you lessons of leadership as you observe how Jesus led His disciples. Study each chapter and reflect on how His example can translate into your marriage relationship.

Evaluate and Get Intentional

Are there ways that you've failed to lead in the past but can begin making new attempts today? Maybe it is in the area of parenting, finances, or spirituality. Ask the Holy Spirit: "How do you want me to start showing leadership?" A few areas that you might consider evaluating are:

Protecting her from chaos: Do you provide leadership in the scheduling of family "rest and recoup" time? Are you providing leadership in directing the course of weekly activities so that you have margins and time available to connect and replenish—or are your lives so full and stretched that you're completely depleted when you get together?

Protecting your marriage from experiencing disconnection: Are you intentional in planning times away with your wife? Whether it's just a luncheon date or a weekend trip, you and your wife need time to connect in an environment that facilitates fresh perspectives. If your wife craves "romantic date nights," demonstrate self-sacrificing leadership by putting forth creative effort to provide that for her.

E: ENTER HER WORLD

It's the Christmas season as we're working on this portion of the book. And you know what that means. Shopping. Lots of shopping. I could easily turn into a hermit during the holidays. I don't like the crowds, the traffic, the sales, but especially the spending. My Kimberly loves all of it. She listens to Christmas music year-round. Seriously. And when this season hits, her excitement and enjoyment is like a child's.

While driving from the mall to Walmart (for the umpteenth time), I'm grasping for patience and attempting to be cheery so that

ENTERING HER WORLD ISN'T ABOUT STRESS AVOIDANCE, IT IS ABOUT TAKING THE INITIATIVE TO KNOW AND PARTICIPATE IN WHAT BRINGS JOY TO YOUR BELOVED.

I don't spoil her joy. She is energized by all the hustle and bustle. I am deflated. She knows shopping is hard for me, and as we drive into the parking lot, she takes pity and insists I stay in the car and listen to "Sports Talk" while she finishes up with her list.

Almost two hours later, I see her coming out with a loaded grocery cart. But there is a problem, not with her, but with the timing. I'm in a dilemma: I wanted to hear the next interview coming up on the radio. Should I keep it on my station or do I turn it back to Burl Ives singing "Frosty the Snowman" for the jillionth time?

Men, this may seem small, but there are times we must enter her world to make her way easier, happier, more enjoyable, and more secure in our love. My wife wouldn't have minded if I'd kept listening to the program, that isn't the point. Entering her world isn't about stress avoidance, it is about taking the initiative to know and participate in what brings joy to your beloved.

I'm not saying you have to get on a first-name basis with the clerk at Bed Bath & Beyond. But there are small ways every husband can show his wife that he cares about what she enjoys, what makes her tick, what brings a sparkle to her eyes, and what makes her feel cared for. Your wife longs for you to enter her world, but most importantly, as you enter her world, you represent Christ to her.

Do you want to demonstrate His love, His heart, His mission? Then we've got to take on His mindset: Jesus did not come to be served; He came to serve and to give His life as a ransom for us (see Mark 10:45). In other words, He entered our world. Literally.

Jesus intentionally became a willing participant in our lives . . . at His own expense. Jesus' coming to earth was not about Him having a better life; it was that we might have life—eternal and abundant.

When you step into your wife's world, you are becoming more Christlike as a husband. Selfish husbands demand that their wives conform to their wishes and adjust their lives accordingly. But the Bible calls for mutual submission, for common respect and deference, and that means entering into each other's worlds.

Listen to Kim convey a wife's perspective, so you can see how much it means for a husband to enter his wife's world:

For years, I felt unloved by LeRoy—because he didn't understand what communicated "love" to me! I tried to convey love to him through the ways that made me feel "loved" and he was doing the same thing to me. I thought hugs and back rubs were the way to his heart—when really he felt more appreciated if I cooked him a pot of brown beans and homemade cornbread. Simple acts of service and words of affirmation convey love to him more than anything else.

The popularity of Gary Chapman's bestselling book *The 5 Love Languages: The Secret to Love That Lasts* is due to the reality that stepping into your spouse's world has real benefits for your marriage. But it took several years before we began to understand the "love language" concept. And in order to know how to demonstrate the specific acts of love that convey to our spouse that we value them, we must enter their world and get to know them.

I sent out a Twitter message, asking wives what they would like to tell their husbands if they could, asking them to give me input for what communicates love to them. One friend sent this response:

"I like when Bob asks about my day. When he asks details and emotions. I love it when he is interested in and cares about things I care about that are not directly part of his life."

Become a student of your wife. Watch what makes her light up. Find out what she likes to read and why. Take a trip with her to her favorite hang-out and listen to her share the stuff that excites her.

Your wife's admiration and respect for you will increase dramatically as you take the time and put forth the effort to actually get to know her. Enter her world and discover more about the woman you love!

Action Steps:

Intentional Involvement

This does not come easily or naturally for most men. Your wife is different from you. Entering her world requires unselfish exertion of time, energy, and sometimes finances. When was the last time that you knowingly, and with purpose, denied yourself in order to bring a small happiness to her by entering her world? It can be costly but the process is an extremely valuable one. Determine today that you will actively engage in the process of entering her world by mapping out a plan of action.

Intelligent Involvement

Live with your wife "according to knowledge" (1 Peter 3:7 KJV). Be alert to her perception of the world. Ask God to help you to "see through her eyes" as much as possible. Take mental note of (and review often) the things your wife delights in, as well as what obviously turns her off. You don't need to know everything perfectly, just pay attention and you'll begin to have a better understanding of her loves (and her love language).

Increased Involvement

Make the attempt. Ask her questions: What is her favorite song currently? What is her favorite color (I hope you already know this!)? What is her favorite Sonic drink? Favorite movie or book and why? Favorite Scripture passage? Favorite date-night spot? What are her greatest challenges currently? Deepest sorrows? Your steps into her world may be awkward at first, and you may think you're failing, but don't give up. Give the effort and God will give you the grace.

The process of entering your wife's world is closely connected to the next component in the P-R-O-T-E-C-T-I-O-N acronym. These two really go hand-in-hand.

C: CHERISH YOUR WOMAN

(LeRoy): One of the most difficult things about working on this book hasn't been spilling my guts publicly, putting in the time and effort to organize and generate the content, or late-night hours on the computer, but the hardest thing has been working on it while struggling physically. I come from a long line of long-living ancestors. My grandparents (on both sides) all lived into their nineties and were relatively healthy until their last breath. My family just doesn't get sick. We don't go to the doctor, because we don't need to. If you're not bleeding, not obviously broken and you're still breathing . . . you just keep going no matter how you feel.

Early in the process of working on this manuscript, I began having some odd physical issues. At first it was occasional bouts with what we came to call my "yuckiness" (our semi-medical terminology). I resisted going to get it checked out. Okay, Kim is working on this portion with me and she wants you to know that I *strongly* resisted getting it checked out.

Men, I love my wife, and I hate to admit it, but resisting her appeals to do something about my health problems was not demonstrating to her that I was cherishing her. And now, as hard as this is for me, I'm fleshing out cherishing her by going through some rigorous medical testing. Some of it is probably a "man thing" but I fought hard against getting on the "medical-merry-go-round." But my beloved wants me around for a few more years, and through this, I've had to

WHEN YOU CAN'T CHERISH YOUR WIFE, YOU NEED A NEW PERSPECTIVE.

admit that cherishing her means getting my health in order. By doing that, it demonstrates to her that she is valuable to me.

We cherish our wives by placing proper value on them. But doing that becomes quite a challenge when our marriage relationship is strained. How is it possible to rightly value your wife when you feel like she doesn't value you at all?

When you can't cherish your wife, you need a new perspective.

In Romans 12:3 we're warned to not think "more highly" of ourselves, or place more value on ourselves, than is right. As husbands, the real hurdle is not to cherish our wives more—but to cherish ourselves less. When we are beat down, despondent, and on the verge of giving up—we can't see clearly. We develop a skewed perspective of ourselves which places a greater value on "me" and lesser value on everyone else—especially our wife. Assigning value is often arbitrary and subjective—so we need something outside of ourselves to provide an accurate perspective.

Clearing the fog and adjusting the lens to see more clearly happens when we place a higher value on God's Word and on Christ. When you lose perspective on God's truth, you lose the ability to properly assign value. It never fails that we eventually "invert" value. Rarely do we ever consciously devalue the currency of Scripture, but when our actions run counter to the Word of God, that is exactly what we're doing. When we don't value our wives, we are actually devaluing Scripture—because Scripture clearly admonishes us to cherish our wife in the same way we cherish our own bodies, and to love her as Christ loves His church (Ephesians 5:28–29).

You and I should value our wife in relation to God's placement of value on her. Your wife holds great value to Him because she is His image bearer. She is valuable because God has a good purpose for her. She is valuable to you and others who her life influences. Her value may have declined in your eyes, but do you believe her value has declined in God's eyes? Ask Him to help you see her value from His perspective.

If you've experienced God's love, how can you fail to show that love to your wife? Are you willing to base her worth on Christ's love for her, rather than basing it on your perspective of her? Before you can lead your wife, you must lead your own heart to follow God, who cherishes her.

Action Steps:

Communicate to Her that She Is Valuable

Go to your wife as soon as you finish reading this chapter (if you can't do it in person now, do it as soon as possible), look her directly in the eyes, and let her know that she matters to you. Say it clearly, firmly, and directly. She needs to know that she matters to you. Some fierce women are convinced that their husband lives in a cave because he doesn't need her, doesn't want to have anything to do with her, is "through" with her. Let your wife know that she matters and is valuable to you. If this brings her to tears (more on emotional meltdowns in the next chapter), don't run, don't let it scare you—just hold her.

She may react by fighting back and venting—telling you, "You sure don't act like I matter to you!" If that's her response, it is a clear indicator that you've tapped into a deep source of pain. Stand strong. Don't run. Ask her forgiveness for not demonstrating it clearly—but let her know that you want to learn how to clearly communicate to her how you value her. You want to understand what her "love language" is, and learn what will convey to her that you care.

Value Her Input

Learning to listen to your wife is an essential element of cherishing her. Your wife may talk a lot, but could it be possible that she keeps dumping voluminous amounts of verbiage on you because you appear to tune her out? She may be talking to get a response from you or some acknowledgment that you hear her, validating her worth. Honor your wife by listening to her. If she tends to unload on you as soon as you walk in the door, and that isn't the best time to have the conversation, gently but clearly convey to her that you want to hear what she has to say, but appeal to set a time that will be more conducive to you being able to give her your undivided attention—and then follow through on that plan.

When facing a decision that will affect you as a couple or family, bring her into the discussion. If you've functioned as a passive man for several years, the problem may not be that you need to "bring her in" but that you need to lead the discussion. She may have "led" the decision-making process for so long that the dynamic needs some major adjustments. If that's the case, you will need to step up to the plate to lovingly explain the need for a change in how decisions are made.

Value Her Expertise

If your wife is a CPA and you flunked basic math courses, don't devalue her abilities to work on the family budget by insisting that "you're the man" and the finances will be under your control (if you're functioning as a passive man, you're probably not giving out that message). Let her know that you appreciate her skills and abilities, don't be jealous of them, but also don't let her successes intimidate or demoralize you—value her for those things. She may struggle with a sense of feeling superior to you in certain areas—which can actually contribute to her insecurity as your wife (and increase her fierceness toward you). In areas where you need to grow and improve, be intentional in increasing your knowledge. You may not know how to replace your microwave, but you can Google it!

Along with valuing her expertise, cherish her by taking responsibility to educate yourself. Don't take the easy route and shift the workload to her just because you're a novice or unknowledgeable. Value her expertise, but don't depend on her to do everything for you—take responsibility for your personal growth (get that math class under your belt!).

Value Her Dreams

Her dreams will probably be different from yours. Ask her about them. Appreciate them. Encourage her in them. Dream together with her. Let this be another way you become a "student" of your wife and learn to live with her "according to knowledge."

> DON'T CONFUSE STUBBORNNESS WITH LEADERSHIP—THEY ARE TWO ENTIRELY DIFFERENT ANIMALS!

Value Her Appeals

Most fierce women don't make appeals, they make demands. But there are times when the passive man actually attempts to "put his foot down" and stubbornly refuses to budge. Don't confuse stubbornness with leadership—they are two entirely different animals! If you hold an opposing opinion that you feel strongly about and she appeals to you to consider her side—listen to her (read the first Action Step again). The two of you can begin to move closer to a united front on an issue as you calmly discuss the pros, cons, and your personal preferences of a difference.

Kim and I have great respect for the theologian Wayne Grudem. You may be familiar with his *Systematic Theology* or other books. I appreciate using his resources, but what I most respect about him is how he lives the theology he teaches. He has written over a hundred pages of scholarly articles on the meaning of the Greek word for "head" in the verse, "The husband is the head of the wife even as Christ is the head of the church" (Ephesians 5:23), but his literal fleshing out of that verse is a beautiful example of cherishing.

Grudem sums up how men are to function as a head: "Leadership while listening with love works out in small family decisions and sometimes large ones . . ."[3]

He was making reference to his decision to move to Arizona. It wasn't a career-building move. At the time (2001), he had been a professor at Trinity Evangelical Divinity School, in Deerfield, Illinois, for twenty years and held the highest rank: Professor with tenure (pretty much guaranteeing him a job for life). He held the chair of the department of Biblical and Systematic Theology, with eight faculty members under him. Trinity has the reputation of being one of the finest academic institutions in the evangelical world. In the prime of his life, while enjoying a successful and prominent teaching career, Dr. Wayne Grudem chose to leave that institution—because he cherishes his wife, Margaret.

Margaret had been experiencing chronic pain for years due to an auto accident, but when they discovered that her pain subsided to some degree when in a drier climate, the Grudems began to pray about a move to Phoenix, Arizona, where Dr. Grudem could teach in a small seminary. In contrast to Trinity's more than fifteen hundred students, Phoenix Seminary had about two hundred students and eight faculty members at that time. God used the Bible passage to husbands to speak to Dr. Grudem about moving for his wife's sake:

> When the day came that I had set apart to consider this before the
> Lord, I opened my Bible to the next passage I would come to in my

regular reading through the Bible, and my eyes fell on Eph. 5:28, "In the same way husbands should love their wives as their own bodies." I thought, "If my body were experiencing the pain that Margaret is experiencing, would I decide to move to Phoenix?" I thought, yes, I would move for the sake of my own body. "Then shouldn't I also move for the sake of Margaret's body?" So I was willing to move, for Margaret's sake.[4]

That is placing the same value on your wife as her Creator places on her. That is cherishing your wife. Grudem's example should instruct us all.

Christ loved you while you were a rebel. Can you love your wife in the same way? You were stumbling in the darkness when Christ came to rescue you. You were without hope and undeserving of God's love, yet He poured it out on you. The noblest act in all of human history was love given when that love was undeserved.

You may have convinced yourself that your wife does not deserve you cherishing her. Did you deserve the love you've been shown? How has God valued and cherished you?

Men, are you cherishing your bride?

⊰ DIGGING IN ⊱

1. Read through the description of the man who actively practices what God delights in: Jeremiah 9:23–24. What three characteristics does this passage list? What would it look like for you to flesh out these in your relationship with your wife?

2. Jesus demonstrates manly leadership throughout the gospel accounts of His life. Just think of the amazing invitation He gave for men of all walks of life to literally "follow" Him. Read through the account of His call to an unlikely convert (Matthew 9:9–13)

and consider the criticism Jesus received because of that. How did Matthew respond to Jesus treating him with the potential to live out a higher calling?

3. What value did Jesus place on Matthew? What value are you placing on your wife? How can you view your wife with the same appreciation that God has for her?

CHAPTER

9

Man to Man

⟶◆⟵

Created to reflect the glory of God, he has retreated sullenly
into his cave—reflecting his own sinfulness.[1]

A. W. Tozer

O ur inboxes are regularly filled with pain. Messages
through social media that are heartbreaking but can also
get my blood boiling. We've been disturbed to find that
the destructive cycle we experienced is far too common. Husbands
and wives are existing as roommates, or worse, as enemies. These
notes, from four different husbands, are just a few of the thousands
of painful lines we've received:

> I need the hammering to stop . . . Divorce is not an option, but my
> wife keeps threatening with one multiple times a year . . . I have two
> young boys and I don't want them to grow up in a broken home, my
> experience of it was not pleasant.

For almost 18 years I have been married to a Fierce Woman, though she was stealthy about it until the last few years . . . pummeled by judgment, condemnation, disapproval, manipulation, inflexibility, gossip, betrayal, and eventually complete detachment . . . this summer, my wife blindsided me by filing for divorce.

Just this morning she told me all of our problems are my fault. I don't know what to do . . . I feel like I'm carrying the weight of our marriage, but I'm sinking alone.

I have done and said so many hurtful things to her, but I believe that she is one of those destructive fierce women. I am still intimidated by her and can't bring myself to tell her that . . . I honestly don't think that she understands that she needs to change.

Four painful messages that represent thousands of broken marriages. Military officers, pastors, and successful CEOs are contacting us asking for help—men who are successful in their careers, but going under fast on the home front. Maybe you could insert your name in one of these anonymous stories.

It's obvious that we need a marital revolution. Men are hurting, women are hurting, and children are caught in their parents' destructive cycle. We're writing this book for you. We're praying that God will break the cycle of pain and we'll see a revolution occur for His glory.

We know you are hurting, but I'm convinced that your wife is hurting as well. There are a lot of fierce women out there who are sheltering deep wounds beneath a tough exterior. Fierce women crying out for love, for protection, for tenderness and leadership. Fierce women who fight back when hit with pain, who lash out to be heard, who hurl insults out of fear, or apply pressure as an enticement for you to prove that you can do more than tuck your tail between your legs.

Have you seen glimpses of your wife as we've walked this journey through these pages?

Have you seen yourself?

Men, this chapter will be a tough read. I'm just warning you before we dive in. Some of this may not apply to you, you may be carrying your full load, but for many of us, we've been guilty of abdicating our manly responsibilities. Get ready—I'm about to unload a truckload of truth on you, man-to-man, so buckle up for the ride.

Let me begin with a tough question:

What if your wife's fierceness is a reaction coming from her deep longing for you to take responsibility as the man?

I'm not excusing her sin. I know it's hard to live with a fierce woman. Believe me, I DO KNOW! But, I also now realize that much of Kim's fierceness was in reaction to my passivity.

It was a vicious cycle: Kim exerted her natural fierce strengths (or opinions, or plans, or commands) and I shrank back in fear— which repulsed her, and she hurled back her fierceness. Sometimes her fierceness just comes out, not as a weapon—but because of her strong personality. She has an intense opinion that must be voiced, she has an urgency that must be acted on, she has a cause that must be fought for, and a conviction that must be felt (by you!).

It helps to remember that the fierce woman is not intending to blow you away with her intensity, it's just who she is. Accepting her beautiful fierceness is part of learning to live with her "according to knowledge" or in an "understanding way" (1 Peter 3:7). Helping her to see how to use her fierce strengths to glorify God is a way you can serve her, not only as her husband, but as her brother in Christ (Galatians 6:1–2).

But if you picked up this book hoping to learn how you could "fix" your fierce wife or how you could "tame the shrew" living under your roof, I hate to disappoint you, but that's not happening here.

You can't fix your wife, in fact that's not part of your job description; God is the only one that can bring true and lasting change to a heart.

You can't fix her—but you can lead her.

You can't change your fierce woman, but what if God is waiting on you to first step up to the plate and take responsibility for your own actions (or lack of them) before He deals with her?

In this chapter, we're closing in on the secret to taking back ground that man lost. Men, reject the temptation to be a wimp. Throw off the urge to go back to bed. Stay the course as you read this next section and we continue working our way through the P-R-O-T-E-C-T-I-O-N acronym. This letter may be the toughest one to digest.

T: TAKE RESPONSIBILITY

She was a new bride, young and in love. She was fierce, but Shaun knew that when he married her. Like most men, he found her fierceness appealing, but now he just found her annoying. He'd long ago checked out. He'd moved on in his heart to what he saw as "grander pursuits"—the virtual realm of battles and glory.

We've heard their story so many times. Different names, but the same story, like this one:

> Early in my marriage (like 1 week after our honeymoon) my husband came home and downloaded an online video game on his computer. This game engulfed his life and our lives. He played around 30-70 hours a week depending on how much time he had off work . . . I begged for affection, sexual and otherwise. I couldn't believe it, married for a few weeks and already going to bed alone.

Marriage contains within it an immediate source for conflict: colliding selfishness. You take two people who are prone to look out for themselves first, before caring for others (aka: two sinners), and you're going to have conflict. Unless you marry at a point of spiritual and emotional maturity, this one issue can be the cause of daily irritations or even weekly explosions. Selfishness leads to blame-shifting (a common characteristic in unhealthy marriages), laziness, faultfinding, a sinfully critical perspective, and a protective mode of operating: "keeping myself soothed and comforted no matter the cost to others."

We've followed Adam's example. God gave him the assignment to provide, to protect, but also to lead spiritually. God gave Adam the clear command to not eat from the tree of the knowledge of good and evil (Genesis 2:15–17), and when Adam failed to take the responsibility to lead and protect his wife, God came looking for him. He confronts His image bearer who is hiding in the bushes: "Have you eaten of the tree of which I commanded you not to eat?" The man said, "The woman whom you gave to be with me, she gave me fruit of the tree, and I ate" (Genesis 3:11–12).

Did you see how quickly Adam shifted the blame to Eve? Throw her under the bus! Yes, she is responsible for her sin, but Adam is justifying his sin by shifting the blame to her. The same scenario has been repeated throughout the centuries. He shifted the blame while failing to confess his failure to protect her.

One way you may have abdicated responsibility is by failing to come alongside your wife and protect her through confronting her in her sin. Yes, I said "confront" her. I know that's a scary thought. I know you may feel you're in no position to speak to her about her "sin," but men, that is the manly and loving thing to do.

Humble confrontation issued out of love, and with the motive of spiritual restoration, is true spiritual leadership. It isn't something to be jumped into without adequate prayer and preparation—but our wives need us to love them well by not ignoring their sin. In the appendix section of the book, you'll find a section titled "Guidelines When Confrontation is Necessary" that I hope you'll prayerfully read and consider.

Confrontation is one of the most loving, but also most difficult, things a fearful husband can do for a fierce wife, but too often most men would rather ignore her sin than risk a war. What we commonly see in counseling couples is that the "Recliner Husband" has replaced the bride's champion of her dreams. He's not willing to risk a war to salvage her soul; he's not even willing to engage with her at all.

FIERCE WIVES TELL US THEY FEEL THEY ARE CARRYING THE BURDEN OF RESPONSIBILITY IN THEIR MARRIAGE.

Recliner Husband has checked out and feels justified in doing so because he's shifted the blame of his pain to her. When a man goes into passive mode, he is sending the message that his wife is not worth fighting for, not worth risking his skin to protect and provide for her.

It may be that he's reached the point of passivity because he's tried so many times and disappointed himself (and her), and believes he'll never improve, can do nothing right, and will always be a loser. He certainly feels he has no legitimacy to be her spiritual leader, much less someone who can confront her. This is when the husband typically checks out . . . checks out to the couch and pulls up some brain numbing activity to soothe the pain and guilt he feels from being a "lazy loser." The warrior has laid down his sword and picked up his remote.

And the destructive cycle goes into a tailspin.

Fierce wives tell us that they feel they are carrying the burden of responsibility in their marriage. Some are carrying the financial burden, the parenting burden, the house-repair burden, the vehicle-care burden, the laundry and meal-prep burden, in addition to the load of a full-time job. If that in any way describes your situation—no wonder your wife is fierce. She is worn out with carrying a weight of responsibility that the two of you should be sharing. At some point, she will unload her wrath. Or she will send out regular messages to you, letting you know how pathetic she thinks you are. She sins. You sin. We have a mess on our hands.

A large percentage of today's men have been raised in a single-parent home, and much of their "training" has come from moms who've had to live independently. You may have entered marriage without ever having an example of a man who took the time or care to prepare you for the responsibilities of marriage. I encourage you to reach out to a spiritually mature man who can help you understand your role but also will help you with practical things you need to learn.

But for others, it isn't that you don't know that you should take responsibility, it is that taking responsibility becomes a source of pain and conflict. And your fear and insecurity can eventually result in procrastination and laziness. You may be the hardest worker you know at your job, but where do you rate with your responsibility to your wife?

Procrastination can be a defense mechanism that we use for personal protection when we're unsure of moving into the unknown or we fear failing again at something we've tried before. We delay to make a decision, or to put into practice a determined course of action, or to apply ourselves to the task at hand, because we fear what might happen. We've failed so many times before, why try again? If we put off working on a solution, the problem will either go away or at least we'll get a temporary break from the stress of worrying about it.

Laziness can result from a prolonged process of procrastination. When the habits of "putting off the hard things" are established—laziness can become the default mode. But the lazy man is different than the procrastinator . . . at least the procrastinator intends to one day complete the task that he knows is his responsibility. Laziness looks to other people to fulfill personal responsibilities. Laziness depends on others rather than exerting self. Indolence is a synonym for laziness and it is derived from the Latin term *indolentia*: "without pain" or "without taking trouble." The lazy man is the man who runs from painful and difficult situations.

I'm not saying that you're lazy, and I'm not here to beat you up. You don't need that. But you may need a gentle push in the right direction. Let me ask you some tough questions, and you make the evaluation: Could it be that your wife views you as fearful and lazy—because you are? You're choosing to give up, because it just seems too hard to keep applying yourself? You're fearful of her, so you've left the conversation, abandoned your areas of responsibility? If so, that will only make things worse.

Men, the answer isn't to run from your duties, but to run toward the hard things.

We see Jesus, the prototype for our role as husbands, "running toward" the hard things when He headed to the cross . . . but we see it way before that dramatic point, we see it in His daily life. Remember the opposition that He continually faced? It seemed to come from the religious community on a regular basis:

> And the scribes who came down from Jerusalem were saying, "He is possessed by Beelzebul," and "by the prince of demons he casts out the demons." (Mark 3:22)

Okay, get the picture. Jesus has been doing what He does best. He's setting captives free, demonstrating God's power, teaching and healing people. So, rather than a pat on the back from His peers, He's accused of being demon possessed, well, actually being possessed by the head of demons. What's His response?

He doesn't run from the problem, doesn't ignore it or delay

dealing with it. Nope, He dives right in to deal with the mess. The very next verse tells us that He calls the scribes to Him . . . He initiates a conversation with them and uses it as an opportunity to teach truth! Jesus is always our example. In this situation, He not only takes responsibility for His actions—He explains what He is doing. Jesus enters into dialogue with those who are opposing Him—but He also uses it as an opportunity to adjust their thinking by pointing them to kingdom truth. Your wife needs you to do that for her.

This may not apply to you. You may be carrying your full load. You may've owned up to your part in your marital dysfunction. You may be doing everything possible to be the godly leader in your home and are taking responsibility for the junk going on there, but if not, don't let this section beat you down . . . don't run to your cave convinced you can never change, that things will never improve, and there's no reason for hope. Go back to the cross. Cry out for God's grace, and know that He is able to provide you with the strength you need to step into every area of responsibility He has for you.

If you want to be respected by your wife, don't run from your responsibilities, but serve her as Christ serves the church. Be the leader, be the man, step up to the plate, and love your wife well.

Action Steps:

Point Your Finger the Other Way

If you've assumed that your wife's fierceness is the whole problem in your relationship, take responsibility for the role you've played in your marital conflicts. Marital conflicts stem from two people—it is never only one person's fault. Stop pointing your finger at her and consider these questions. Have you been passive? Have you retreated? Have you been lazy? Admit it. Take responsibility and let her know that you're not going to hide in the bushes any longer. You're making the tough choice to come out in the open and deal with the issues. Let her know that you're not going to abandon her or leave her to deal with your junk.

Take Out the Trash

I mean this literally. Do you take out the trash at your house? Do you deal with the messy stuff? I'm speaking both literally and metaphorically. Your mom may've been the one to take out the trash at your house, but I want to challenge you to take on the messy jobs; don't leave it to your wife to do. And not just the literal trash, but the mess that's happening in your home right now.

Are you leaving all the dirty jobs to your wife to deal with? The leaky faucet, the complaining neighbor, the car maintenance, the home-repair projects that you keep ignoring? Ask your wife what projects she'd like for you to take ownership of. If you don't know how to do it (can't figure it out after using Google), get a friend involved or pay a repairman.

Don't grumble and complain when she asks for your help; don't heave a heavy sigh and get angry when she waves her "honey-do" list in your face (again). And especially, don't leave all the work to your wife! If there's work to be done, responsibilities to be carried, decisions to be made—don't leave her to shoulder what should be yours. If there is a dispute between her and the children—get engaged, don't sit on the sidelines and watch them battle it out. Stand up for her, provide and protect her—be her champion.

Love Her Enough to Confront

Your wife's fierce tendencies may be her personality type, but the way she expresses her fierceness may be sinful. Love her enough to come alongside her and care for her soul. Check out the "Guidelines When Confrontation is Necessary" included in the appendix.

John and Krista looked like Ken and Barbie when they married. After decades of ups and downs, their three daughters were out of the house, one in college, one married, and one starting a career, and Krista, for the first time since high school, had loads of free time—and she was enjoying it. John's job took him out of town through much of the week and Krista was lonely. Empty house, empty bed, long nights. It wasn't long before a coworker noticed Krista's loneliness.

What began as a friendly connection led to passionate nights in bed together while John was out of town. Krista never dreamed how quickly her heart could turn from her husband and be tied completely to another man, but it felt like she couldn't live without him. When the affair came into public view, Krista wanted to end her life. Wanted to run. Wanted to hide. But John wouldn't let her.

John stepped up to serve her as never before, and stood for her through the public humiliation and pain. He not only forgave her, but he asked her forgiveness for failing to be the spiritual leader she needed. He took responsibility for his failure.

John made some practical changes with his job that cost him financially, but allowed him to be home more. They entered an intense season of counseling. John became intentional in praying with Krista and leading her through Scripture studies. He was outspoken about his failure as a husband and took responsibility for his part in the issues that contributed to Krista's affair. God mercifully healed this marriage. It hasn't been easy. It has been hard. But it has been good. Their marriage stands today as a public trophy of God's grace and redemption.

We've seen God do amazing things in marriages that looked

beyond hope—but the real key is the husband taking spiritual responsibility for his wife's soul. Let your wife know that you're not going to let her continue down a path of destruction—you're going to step up to take responsibility.

And now men, we've reached the most personal aspect of the P-R-O-T-E-C-T-I-O-N acronym. Things may get a little uncomfortable and hit pretty close to home, but if you're still with me after the last hard-hitting section, then I think you'll be glad you hung in here for this. We're talking about oneness; intimacy in all three aspects: emotional, spiritual, and physical. And it is no accident that this section follows the last. You will not experience oneness if you fail to take responsibility.

I: INTIMATE CONNECTIONS

Kim's mom became a widow at seventy-two years old and after a year of deep grieving she began hanging out with old classmates— one of whom was a widowed pastor. They had been friends since high school and he even assisted in Kim's dad's funeral, so her mom and J. B. Evans had a long history together. J. B. and Annette started hanging out more often than just at class reunions and large gatherings. The more time they spent together, the more they enjoyed each other. And they laughed a lot. Eventually their friendship led them down the wedding aisle.

The emotional connection is what often strikes the first spark between a couple. It's good to start out as friends and let that friendship grow and thrive. The bond of deep friendship isn't easily breached. If you can count your wife as your closest friend, you are a blessed man. If you and your wife are functioning more as combatants than friends—it's time to call a truce and work on rediscovering what first drew you to each other. It's time to laugh together again.

Friendship thrives when integrity, loyalty, and unselfishness

characterize your relationship. When you have those three components in place and work at appreciating your differences (entering
her world) while finding common interests that you can regularly
enjoy together, friendship becomes a strong bond for the marriage
relationship.

Making the Emotional Connection

Connecting with your wife on an emotional level can be a real challenge for men who tend to be nonemotional. In fact, for some of
us, we typically take Sgt. Joe Friday's approach on the old TV show:
"Just give me the facts, Ma'am." Some men are more "Vulcan" than
human, and agree with Mr. Spock's opinion: "I find their illogic and
foolish emotions a constant irritant." But part of the commitment to
live with your wife "in an understanding way" is to recognize (and
appreciate) that she is an emotional creature and laughter and tears
come easily for her.

For most of us, tears can shut us down. They scare us. We don't
know what to do with them. Tears were usually my signal to take off
and hide. If the tears started after we were both in bed, that was time
for me to start snoring. But Kim explained to me that tears are actually the woman's way of alerting you to the fact that she is in need. She
needs your reassurance that everything is going to be all right, that you
are alert to her concerns, that you care, that you value her pain. Tears
can be a cry for comfort, for validation, and for affirmation. Tears can
be signaling the fact that you are not demonstrating compassion.

But Kim wants me to warn you that tears can also be a manipulative
device, so it is important to have a healthy discussion with your wife
and get to the source of her tears. Is she crying so you will give in to her
appeals after you've made a tough leadership decision that she disagrees
with? To wear you down? To stir your emotions? To get unhealthy pity?

When a woman reaches the emotional tipping point of a

meltdown, that is probably not the best time to have the discussion to get to the root issue of what is causing the tears. Instead, this is the time when you need to hold her while she cries and voice a verbal appeal to the Father. Pray over her, pray for her, value her by interceding for her (out loud) as she weeps.

Developing the One-Souled Relationship

Listen to this charge from the apostle Paul and think about it in relation to building a healthy emotional and spiritual relationship with your wife:

"Make my joy complete by being of the same mind, maintaining the same love, **united in spirit**, intent on one purpose" (Philippians 2:2 NASB, emphasis added).

"*United in spirit*" literally means "*one-souled.*" Because of the unity that comes from abiding in Christ, believers are the only people in the world who can experience **one-souled relationships**. God wants this to typify every relationship within the body of Christ, but especially in your marriage. The emotional is tied closely to the spiritual. If the Holy Spirit lives within each of you, then you have the same Person within who can unite you spiritually and emotionally.

Throughout the book, I've been challenging you to be the spiritual leader in your marriage. When you take on that role, you are laying the necessary foundation for you and your wife to experience spiritual oneness. Since I've covered that topic on several pages, I'm not going to spend a lot of time rehashing that in this chapter. But, one thing you should know as a man, you should cherish your wife enough to love her soul more than you love her body. Don't grab your wife for sex if you're not willing to take her hand and pray for her.

> DON'T GRAB YOUR WIFE FOR SEX IF YOU'RE NOT WILLING TO TAKE HER HAND AND PRAY FOR HER.

Cultivate Holy Pleasure

One of the most enjoyable and sacred gifts God gives to a couple is the sensual enjoyment of physical intimacy. God intends for you and your wife to experience holy pleasure and delight through the sexual relationship and in that, you can bring Him glory. Because your delight in each other glorifies God, it only stands to reason that the sexual relationship would be a primary target of the enemy. The physical act of oneness is not only a means of procreation (and the enemy *hates* new life), but it's also the pleasurable avenue through which the marital couple can experience the most intimate physical union possible (and the enemy *hates* marital unity). When a couple is united emotionally, spiritually, and physically—watch out, there's real power there!

But the fact of the matter is that many couples are broken and hurting in the area of physical intimacy. There is a high percentage of fierce women who've been violated sexually. Your wife may've experienced the horrors of sexual abuse and never even shared that with you. She may be geared to "fight" back and repulsed by the thought of sexual encounters with you—not because of you, but because of her past wounding.

If you and your wife have difficulty in this area, be prayerful and consider the possibility that she may have past issues that are preventing her from experiencing freedom and joy. Be prayerful about opening up a conversation and providing a safe place for her to share, in case she needs to confide in you anything from her past that she's hidden from you.

A lack of sexual desire and activity is a common characteristic that we've seen in the Fierce Women/Fearful Men cycle. Not only from a wife experiencing violation in the past, but from husbands being fearful in the present. When we're failing in every aspect of our relationship with our wife, the last thing we men want to do is fail in this department, too!

So, we have a few sinful options: become celibate, gratify ourselves immorally through masturbation, porn, or sexual affairs. At the same time that we're seeking sinful gratification, we aren't meeting our wife's sexual needs, so she is tempted to reach out to someone or something else to fulfill those desires. Plenty of fierce women are fully engaged in church activities, while also fully engaged in a sexual affair. The church is packed with this kind of immorality.

You may not struggle with this, but I'm confessing to you, in those dark years where I felt like no matter what I did, I could do nothing right—the last thing I wanted to do was to snuggle up close to the woman who intimidated me. Failing to be the man in the bedroom was just one more thing I didn't want to add to my list. So I pulled away from Kim sexually.

Some men can disconnect their emotions from their sexual encounters (which isn't a healthy thing), but I couldn't. The best course of action would've been to work on getting things right with her, Scripturally we aren't to neglect our wives sexually (1 Corinthians 7:3). But for men who already see themselves as failures and are intimidated in every way by their wives, the sexual arena is one power play we can hold on to.

Porn and self-gratification will be a strong enticement when you turn away from your wife. Unfaithfulness through an affair, giving her the cold shoulder in the bedroom, or even workaholic behavior, provides a sense of being able to have some kind of "control" in your life. You may not be able to win with your wife, but at least you can "win" here.

We looked at the tendency to abdicate our responsibility in the first half of this chapter, and leaving your wife out in the cold sexually is another form of neglect. Now, admittedly, you can't force yourself into arousal with your wife, but this is why it is so important to begin the process of bringing down the walls that divide you emotionally and spiritually before you work on this area of your relationship. As you begin to build a healthy relationship in those two areas, the physical desire for your wife will return (unless you're having a medical issue that needs to be checked out). I assure you, God desires (and provides the grace and help) for you and your wife to experience intimacy at every level.

Action Steps:

Talk to Your Wife about Her Needs

You may not believe this, but your wife needs you. She does. She may put off an air of superiority, may function independently, and may refuse your help too often, but she does need you—more than she yet realizes. Talk to her about what emotional, spiritual, and physical needs she has that you aren't fulfilling. Be ready for a strong response to this question and be open to her suggestions. If she comes out swinging (from years of repressed yearning), take a dive—and then gently, but firmly, lead her to a place of calm by explaining to her that you truly want to work on these three areas, but you need her help. You need her to help you by speaking calmly and being open to understanding the challenges you have with intimacy. If you've failed her in the past, don't excuse or justify your sin, confess it and ask for her forgiveness. But also, ask her to understand and help you as you attempt to grow in these three areas.

Schedule Some Fun

You may not be a planner, and spontaneity is a beautiful thing, but be intentional to set up an opportunity for the two of you to do something you both enjoy (something that requires interaction—no vegging out or just sitting in front of the TV all night).

Play a board game, cook a meal together, hike a mountain trail, go to a museum. If you can afford it, go to a hotel and spend the day in bed together snacking, sleeping, laughing, and loving on each other. You plan it, and that will communicate to her that she's worth the effort. Plan to use this time to build intimacy in all three areas.

Evaluate and Articulate Your Needs

Let your wife know how you're naturally wired (your emotional, spiritual, and physical makeup). Don't assume that she knows this already. Whether you're an introvert or an extrovert, talk about what that means and be honest about how you're tempted with sinful expressions of that personality trait. Share with her how she can help you to function with your particular personality in healthy non-sinful ways. If you're frustrated with your sexual relationship, let her know that (in a gentle and non-slamming way). If you've sinned against her sexually, confess that and seek her forgiveness, after you've studied the "Guidelines for Restoration" in the appendix portion of the book. You will not be able to have marital unity if you are sinning against your wife. Period.

One of the most dramatic illustrations of marital restoration that we've experienced was when we walked with a young couple through his confession and repentance of a homosexual affair that he'd been secretly involved in for several years. He'd reached a miserable and suicidal state, believing he'd never get victory over his temptation to sin against his wife. That hidden sin made it impossible for them to experience the joy and freedom of marital unity. When the husband reached out to confess to me, the first chains of bondage began to loosen. Then, as we went together for him to confess to his wife (who had no clue of his double life), he experienced true freedom and deliverance. God moved into their lives in an incredible way, as the enemy no longer had a stronghold when repentance and confession brought everything into the light. God mercifully gave his wife the grace to forgive him and a heart to begin building their marriage on truth rather than lies. It was a long road of recovery, but the outcome was a transforming work of grace.

Nothing is worth hanging on to that would prevent you and your wife from enjoying deep intimacy at every level!

☙ Digging In ❧

1. We see several instructions in Ephesians 5:1–21 that apply to our chapter. As an "imitator of God" what does taking responsibility look like as it relates to your relationship with your wife?

2. "Walking in love" includes humble confrontation of your wife's sin. Read and pray through the "Guidelines When Confrontation is Necessary" in the appendix. Is there an area where your wife is struggling? What would it look like to demonstrate love to her rather than ignoring her sin?

3. As you read through the passage in Ephesians 5, consider whether you need to confess sexual immorality and seek God's forgiveness. Use the "Guidelines for Restoration" in the appendix for help with your next steps if you've sinned sexually against your wife. Do you have another man who is willing to hold you accountable and serve as a brother to help you in your battle with this?

Never Go AWOL

❖

Far better it is to dare mighty things, to win glorious triumphs,
even though checkered by failure, than to take rank with those
poor spirits who neither enjoy nor suffer too much, because
they live in the gray twilight that knows not victory nor defeat.[1]

THEODORE ROOSEVELT

I dug as low into the grass as my face could press. I'm not a "crier"
but, to be honest, I released it all, soaking the ground into a
muddy hole. I felt abandoned by God. Felt totally alone and
rejected. My torment seemed unwarranted. Then God did something I didn't deserve. He spoke. He opened my eyes. He allowed me
to understand. In my pain, He shouted.

We've taken the last four chapters to walk through the P-R-O-T-
E-C-T-I-O-N acronym and now, we reach the last two letters of our
assignment. Men, I'm challenging you to finish well. To press into your
pain so you can hear. To stay the course and see what God will do.

O: OPEN YOUR HEART

Are you listening? Are you watching? Are you open to the lessons God has for you in this dark and painful season? Sometimes it seems God is silent, but what we don't realize is: God has been speaking to us, preparing us, although quietly, long before we reach the point of crisis.

C. S. Lewis had a keen understanding of how God speaks: "We can ignore even pleasure. But pain insists upon being attended to. God whispers to us in our pleasures, speaks in our conscience, but shouts in our pains: it is his megaphone to rouse a deaf world."[2]

When I was a young man, I heard a message at a Bible conference that was confusing to me. The preacher was Ron Dunn and his message corresponded with nothing I'd previously known or understood about God. Theologically, the message was solid, and in my heart, the Holy Spirit confirmed the truthfulness of his preaching. But the problem for me, in listening to him, was that I had nothing in my life experience that could help me connect the dots. His message was entitled "Strange Ministries." He taught through several Scriptures to make the point that God uses unlikely and unwelcome "teachers" in our lives. These "strange ministries" teach us about God and His ways in a manner that we could not otherwise know Him.

That's been more than thirty years, but I still remember some of his points. The ministry of fear. The ministry of weakness. The ministry of failure. The ministry of suffering. I didn't realize it then, but God was whispering to my heart truth that I would need for lessons that I would not learn until years later. God was speaking to me as a single young man who'd encountered few trials and He was preparing me, way back then, for the dark season of pain that He knew I would face in my marriage. He was preparing me to see God more clearly in the darkness.

God doesn't typically shout through a megaphone when He

communicates, but He quietly, even secretly, prepares us for the hard things He knows we will face. He instructs us even when we're unaware that we're being taught (or that we need to be taught). Even when we're deafened by our pain and blinded by the darkness, He is working, He is instructing our hearts. He often whispers so softly that we can't understand what He's saying, until the painful journey reveals His kind intentions and reminds us of timely truth that He's already imparted. He is speaking to you now, are you open to hear?

You may feel like God has abandoned you and that you're wandering aimlessly through the darkness. At times, God uses the darkness to hide, so that when He chooses to reveal Himself, we understand Him in a way we could not have otherwise known Him. When you're in the darkness, it is hard to be open to the lessons God wants to teach you. Most days you're just trying to survive. When you fail (once again) in your wife's eyes, you're probably not going to gladly receive a message on "How failure can produce blessing."

You've probably read Job's words "I had heard of you by the hearing of the ear, but now my eye sees you" (Job 42:5). The context of Job's statement was suffering. Job had only "heard of God" but his understanding was limited, and God was hidden from his view. When the hammer of suffering strikes its cruel blows, the whisperings of God can be heard more clearly. The whisperings become shouts and give way to clear comprehension. Truths we had previously taken for granted, become life sustaining. I've encountered God this way. Perhaps, at this moment, you hear some of the whispers of God— reminding you of truth already known, but lessons yet to be learned.

It may be hard for you to hear God speaking right now, but I encourage you to open your heart to anything and everything God desires to communicate to you. Looking back, the truths I desperately needed were the very same truths God had already planted in my heart. When those truths were watered with the tears of brokenness and pain, those truths became a garden where God met with me. God's timing is perfect. When He plants seeds of truth in our lives, He will bring about a harvest of righteousness in His perfect time, as we respond to His work.

During the darkest seasons of our marriage, I would have scoffed at the idea of learning anything beneficial while in such a miserable place or that anything good could come from such pain. I could not have been more wrong. God gave me "treasures" in the darkness.

"I will give you the treasures of darkness and hidden wealth of secret places, so that you may know that it is I, the Lord, the God of Israel, who calls you by your name" (Isaiah 45:3 NASB).

A difficult marriage is not the way any of us would choose to know God more intimately or understand His Word more clearly. But God is always faithful to do exactly what is necessary in order that His perfect will can be accomplished in our lives. Nancy DeMoss Wolgemuth has wisely said: "God's will is what we would choose if we knew what God knows." God's intention is to bring treasures out of your darkness.

> IT MAY BE THAT GOD WORKS IN SECRET BECAUSE HE DOESN'T WANT US TO GET IN THE WAY.

A miserable marriage is not God's perfect will, but God is so wise and so awesome in power that He alone can take the worst and work out His best for His eternal glory. For anyone who was watching the darkness and suffering that Christ endured on the cross, they would've thought Jesus' state was hopeless. Little did they realize that the cross was actually the point of His greatest victory. What crushed Him became the doorway to eternal life—for us all. God brought "treasures"—eternal treasures, out of that darkness!

As men, we like to have things under our control; we need to know what's happening and what's coming, so we can be ready to handle anything thrown our way. We expect God to clue us in on His agenda, but that's not how God usually works; He doesn't let us in on everything He's doing. When He so chooses, He works secretly.

God works in secret and does not have to prove Himself to us. He will not dance to our tunes or turn at our whim. He does not owe us an explanation of His secret work. It may be that God works in secret when He doesn't want us to get in the way.

God works in secret so that His revelations may bring Him greater glory. At times He works secretly, preventing us from seeing that He is at work, to mature us. When we are able to look back and see that He was working all along, our praise will be sweeter, our faith stronger, and our understanding of Him clearer. Even in eternity God will remain, in some sense, unknowable. He is utterly transcendent, perfectly ineffable.

I don't know all that God is teaching you. I do know He longs for you to draw near to Him. I know it may seem like there is nothing good that can come from this. You might be asking, "God, what are You doing through all of this?" The fact is you may not know until years have passed. I am convinced there are some mysteries that only the clear light of eternity will reveal. One day you will understand God's purposes and everlasting praise will be your response.

Action Steps:

Intentionally Listen

Set aside a period of time where you will have no interruptions, and allow God to speak to you. You will need to take with you a legal pad (or two), a Bible, and nothing else (unless directed by the Lord). Turn your phone on silent. Spend time praying; asking God to speak to you through His Word. Trust the Holy Spirit to provide leadership in the passages you should read. Ask the Holy Spirit to bring to mind truths you may have learned in the past but have faded from memory over time. Consider fasting during this time and be prepared to wait on the Lord. Read God's Word ... pray ... wait and repeat.

Intentionally Search

Seek God's direction for resources, people, or opportunities that He desires to use in maturing you through this season: specific books (those you may have read in the past or those you have not read), special people (those you presently know or those you do not yet know), spiritual encounters (Christian conferences, blog sites, revivals, men's meetings and prayer groups).

Intentionally Serve

Focus on others. Look for ways to serve others (starting with your wife). Myopia—not being able to see beyond yourself—is a common malady when going through trials. Find ways to be a blessing to others who are also struggling. This is crucial in keeping your heart from hardening. If you've already lost the ability to feel compassion for others, you are in a dangerous place spiritually. Seek godly counsel immediately.

Intentionally Surrender

Accept God's timing. Don't attempt to force God's hand (never a good idea). Let patience have her perfect work (James 1:4). Ask for "mushroom grace" (the ability to grow spiritually in a very dark place). Let God know that whatever He wants to do in your heart is what you desire more than anything. Tell the Lord His timing is perfectly acceptable to you. Relay your utter confidence in Him regardless of outcomes contrary to your perception of what is best.

If you will open your heart to the lessons that God wants you to learn, He will prepare you for what lies ahead. He will give you the grace, joy, and power to step out of the darkness and into the light. He will give you the endurance to stay the course for the long haul.

We've reached the final letter of the P-R-O-T-E-C-T-I-O-N acronym. How you respond to the message in this section of the book will determine whether you check out of the race before reaching the finish line. Whether you stay in the battle to the end or go AWOL. How you choose will determine how you will finish.

N: NEVER GIVE UP

Lieutenant General William G. Boykin served for thirty-six years in the United States Army. He is a former commander of Delta Force, an elite group of soldiers who served under him in Special Operations. In 1993, two of his men sacrificed their lives in the Blackhawk Down rescue effort in Mogadishu, Somalia. I appreciate his commitment to excellence and his sacrifice for our nation. His charge clarifies what we need, as men, to never give up:

"Each man must determine what is dear to him and what is worth sacrificing for. A transcendent cause must exist in a man's life if he is to reach his full potential as a man. Few men today have done a thorough self-analysis to ascertain what their transcendent cause is—or even if they have one. It is time, though: time to determine what we hold dear and what is worthy of sacrifice. As men, we cannot wait . . . I urge you: do it now, and bring meaning to who you are as a man."[3]

Do you understand the transcendent cause that your marriage represents? We'll share more about that in the next chapter, but right now, I want you to consider—does your marriage matter beyond how it affects you and your family? More than your own happiness? I assure you, it does.

The battle for your marriage is a battle that has transcendent implications. Your willingness to pick up your sword and take your stand—no matter how fierce the opposition—is at the heart of manhood. This is the battle God is calling you to fight—the battle for God's honor and glory to be seen in your marriage! Let me transport you back in time to a little known victory accomplished by a man fighting for a transcendent cause. He lived to serve His God and was willing to lay down his life to secure a victory for His honor:

On a rocky outcropping of a Judean hillside, a lone sentinel crouches under a scrub cedar. Shammah scans the boulders and bushes in the valley beneath him. The cold wind stings his weathered face as he strains to hear any sound of an approaching enemy. Immediately to his left—a small patch of lentils is nestled on a terraced plot that slopes gently upward to the edge of a limestone bluff. In this barren wilderness, even a small patch of peas is worth guarding.

They were just peas. Not very tasty. Not much nutritional value. Not enough to feed many. But they were God's peas intended for consumption by God's people. They were the property of the God of Israel. The noble soldier was one of David's loyal friends—Scripture refers to him as one of David's "mighty men" (2 Samuel 23:8–12).

Standing guard, Shammah thinks about the many times he had come to the aid of his king. The bloody horror of battle giving way to shouts of victory, as he and his companions celebrated as warriors do. But this day, he isn't headed out to fight a mighty battle. He serves in a small assignment—guarding a small pea patch—but Shammah determined he would give his all to fulfill his simple responsibility for that day.

A snapped twig, and the scree of loose shale under an approaching sandal, commands his full attention. All of his battle-hardened senses immediately rise to high alert. His keen eyesight picks up a slight movement in the tree line about a hundred paces below him and to his right. He remains perfectly still . . . hardly breathing, ready for anything, afraid of nothing.

He silently lifts a prayer to Jehovah, Lord of hosts, asking for strength to serve Him in the danger he senses is coming. As he asks God to grant him victory for His glory, he spots stealthily advancing enemies. From his vantage point, Shammah sees a large band of Philistine soldiers approaching. They are coming for this patch of lentils.

Shammah sounds the alarm, but rather than preparing for battle, his men all run for their lives. They take off; go AWOL in the face of this fierce horde. The realization makes his knees weak—he has two choices: quietly slip away, or stay and stand his ground; do his duty and fight . . . defending God's pea patch alone.

He chooses the latter. Shammah knows the implications of that choice. It could be the last decision he would ever make. If it is to be the will of his God, he resolves to die with honor. He will stand, fight, suffer, bleed, and die if called upon to do so—but he will not desert his post, abdicate his responsibility, or flinch in the face of fierce adversity. He will keep to his assignment, and he will fight for God's glory.

When he stands, exposing his position to the enemy, there is no turning back, no fighting from the periphery, or taking puny potshots with a sling. This courageous warrior runs to meet his adversaries in deadly combat. Standing in the middle of the pea patch, this solitary man takes on all comers, defending God's lentils and God's honor.

One by one, the enemy goes down under the blade of his sword. When the last Philistine falls, Shammah also falls—to his knees, bloody, bruised, and exhausted, worshiping the God of Israel, the God who hears the humble prayers of weary, lonely soldiers.

When a detachment of Israel's finest charge over the ridge, the battle picture shocks them. One man standing alone, in the peas, surrounded by a troop of once mighty Philistines, now all fallen corpses. One lone man determined to fight for his transcendent cause—God's glory above all else.

Shammah's heroic victory became legendary among Israel's fighting men. His strength, resolve, faith, and commitment to seeing his responsibility through to the end, encouraged generations of young men to take their stand in battle—even when alone and outnumbered. Shammah is a witness to the grace of God given to a man who decides he will not run or flee but remains at his post whatever the cost to him personally.[4]

Shammah is an example to us all. You might prefer facing a horde of fierce Philistines than to face your fierce wife, but the fact is—battling for your marriage has much greater implications than any physical battle you could engage in. Today we live in a "disposable marriage" culture and divorce is a convenient option, but for the courageous soldier, divorce is not an option.

When speaking at marriage conferences, I joke that I've told Kim, "You can leave me if you choose to, but I'm coming with you!" Actually, divorce was never an option for either of us; we both held so strongly to a belief in the sanctity of making a covenant with God when we married, that we were committed to living in misery . . . to the death, if necessary, but we would not divorce. That's not really a noble commitment, that's noble misery. In the early days, our commitment to "sticking together" was stronger than our confidence that God could bring transformation to our marriage.

You may be thinking, "I haven't gone AWOL, I'm still here, haven't left her . . ." You may still live under the same roof—but have you walked away emotionally? Have you checked out? If you aren't actively battling for joy and unity in your marriage—then you've gone AWOL.

You may be yelling at me, I can't do this alone, it takes two to make a marriage work, ya know? You're right. You can't do this alone, you must have the Author of marriage leading, impressing, directing your heart. You and He can impact your relationship with your wife. You have His word on that. He doesn't hold out false hope. In fact, He anticipated that you would need this passage for this exact moment in your life:

> For this reason I bow my knees before the Father, from whom every family in heaven and on earth is named, that according to the riches of his glory he may grant you to be strengthened with power through his Spirit in your inner being, so that Christ may dwell in your hearts through faith—that you, being rooted and grounded in love, may have strength to comprehend with all the saints what is the breadth and length and height and depth, and to know the love of Christ that surpasses knowledge, that you may be filled with all the fullness of God.

> Now to him who is able to do far more abundantly than all that we ask or think, according to the power at work within us, to him be glory . . . (Ephesians 3:14–21)

What is the answer to your problem?

The answer is the heart.

A heart that's lost all hope is a dead heart and a woman can sense that a mile away.

Neither of you will be able to enjoy the life you share if your hope has died.

Do you believe that God is able to do far more than you can "ask or think" in regard to reaching your wife's heart? Do you believe God can impact your wife?

Maybe your wife has a relationship with God, but the relationship between the two of you is shadowed by betrayal, broken promises, shattered dreams, or just empty space. She may be one fierce woman—but not even realize it, or be willing to consider it, or if she knows that she's fierce, she may actually be proud of it. And you see no hope for things ever changing or improving.

You can resign yourself to this, or you can believe

You can believe that God's Word is true and one plus One can make a difference. You can believe that because of the gospel—there is still reason for hope. You can admit that—by losing hope—you've settled for less than what God can do, and ask God for forgiveness.

Do you believe that He supplies the power that is needed to transform you, your wife, and your marriage? Have you become skeptical? How does that line up with the power and ability for God to work that is described in the Ephesians passage?

In order to embrace this battle, you need more than sheer willpower, you need hope for victory and you need to understand the transcendent implications for this battle (we'll talk more about that in the next chapter). Without the hope and confidence that God can provide, you will remain in that lonely and defeated position.

I lived in hopelessness for years. It affected my job, my relationship with my children, my outlook on life—everything. I remained in a dark depression until I faced the fear and picked up the mantle of manhood to get back into the race. I shudder to think about where I would be today, and all the joy we would've missed out on, if I had remained in hiding.

We have a friend who decided to run the Greek Marathon late in life. The Greek Marathon is a rigorous course of difficult hills, and a little over twenty-six miles, leading to the finish line at the historic Panathenaic Stadium in Athens. Although he'd never run this race before, it had been a dream earlier in his life, and when Sammy was diagnosed with cancer, he determined to run the marathon.

Sammy had cancer surgery before he began training for the race and at sixty-one he stepped onto the track to begin the grueling run that has taken more than one life. In fact, although he completed the marathon, he had to be transported to the hospital right after he finished the race, but he was released shortly afterward. His determination and the goal of completion drove him through the months of training and prepared him to meet the most ambitious physical challenge of his life. Seconds after crossing the finish line, just before collapsing, Sammy told a reporter:

"This was the most difficult thing I have ever done in my life. I didn't run as fast as I had hoped. But I came to a place in the race where speed was not the most important thing, but finishing the race was all that mattered."[5]

Sammy had his eyes set on the goal. Finishing the race.

Can you set your eyes on the goal? The goal isn't to have a life free from pain or conflict. The goal isn't even winning your wife's love and affection—you can follow every action step in this book, and it will not guarantee that (and that shouldn't be your motive, by the way). The goal is for you to stand guard, protecting what God has entrusted to you, to serve your wife and your God as a faithful soldier. No matter the outcome, no matter the opposition, to stand as a man who reflects the image of his Creator and his Savior. Your goal is to be the man God created you to be, and your motivation for doing that is your love for Christ.

Action Steps:

Adopt a Battle Mentality

View your marriage, not as a battle, but as something you must battle to protect. Rather than viewing your wife as your enemy, look for ways to draw her into this conflict—as your ally. Talk to her about the need for the two of you to unite in the goal of protecting your marriage relationship. Begin with agreeing to remove the word "divorce" from your marriage vocabulary. Lovingly share with your wife the importance of not using divorce as a threat in conversation or as a fantasy in private. If your wife has already filed for divorce or you are currently separated, don't let that prevent you from attempting reconciliation (unless she has remarried). Don't let the present circumstances shake the resolve of your heart to battle for your marriage.

Enter the Sacred Covenant

Consider planting a "marker in the ground" or setting a "memorial stone" by writing out a document that describes the marriage covenant and your determination to commit to this sacred union—for life. Take time preparing this, pray and search the Scriptures to write out a descriptive statement (personalized for you and your wife) that conveys the sacred bond that holds your marriage, and the covenant with God that you entered into at your wedding. This may be something you would want to do in conjunction with a vow renewal ceremony.

Seek Out Accountability

Share with a spiritually mature couple the struggles that you've had in your marriage and your desire to protect your relationship. Ask the couple if they would be willing to spend time with you regularly, for enjoyable fellowship, but also for the sake of accountability. Let them know that you are inviting them into your lives and giving them permission to ask hard questions and that you will be receptive to their biblical counsel. Share with this couple the commitment to remove divorce as an option and ask them to help you and your wife remain true to that vow.

The portrait of marriage that you'll find in the next chapter will provide you with that "transcendent cause" to fight for as you seek to practically apply the Action Steps of this chapter. As you continue to press into this journey, I want to encourage you that the battle you are waging is well worth the effort you will expend. A God-glorifying relationship with your wife is worthy of your personal sacrifice.

⊰ DIGGING IN ⊱

1. Jesus came with the determination to spill His blood on the cross as the atoning sacrifice for our sinful condition. The road to the cross was grueling, but He didn't allow anything to deter Him from His mission (refer back to chapter 1, "Digging In"). What was Jesus' response to Peter's rebuke when he opposed His commitment to the cross (Matthew 16:13–28)? To whom did Jesus attribute this plan to avoid the cross?

2. Jesus provides His philosophy for His mission to earth in John 4:34 and sums up His work in John 19:30. After reading those Scriptures, consider His example of perseverance as you read 1 Peter 2:21–24. What is your philosophy of perseverance for marriage? Can you articulate that to your wife? I encourage you to write out your philosophy for marriage and refer to it often.

3. As the apostle Paul awaits execution, he sends final words to his son in the faith. Read his powerful farewell message and allow this to encourage you as you persevere: 2 Timothy 4:6–8.

What's the Big Deal about Marriage, Anyway?

❖

If marriage is a picture of Christ and His love for His church,
then much more is at stake than my happiness. The world should
long for what Christians have. If our marriages aren't filled with
kindness and joy, why would anyone want what we offer?
But when they see in us a mutual delight, a gentle and easy trust
in one another, they can't help but ask, "What's your secret?"[1]

HERSHAEL YORK
(Professor of Preaching at Southern Baptist Theological Seminary)

The question of the day is not "What's your secret?" but is
"What's the big deal about marriage, anyway?" With the
growing percentage of couples choosing to live together
before marriage and the "redefining" of marriage by our culture, it
is obvious that the purpose for marriage has been lost. Marriage is
suffering under the selfish pursuit of modern-day man.

When people watch your marriage, what do they see? Do they
see an example of the love that exists between Christ and His bride,

the church? Maybe on the outside you look fine. Maybe no one in your church is aware of the pain and estrangement, but if your marriage is caught in the "Fierce Women/Fearful Men" cycle, it is probably obvious to others that your relationship isn't a pleasant one.

WHEN PEOPLE WATCH YOUR MARRIAGE, WHAT DO THEY SEE?

In the last chapter, we challenged you to hang in there, to press on, to never go AWOL, and we told you that marriage matters—beyond your own happiness. But our culture has reached the place where personal happiness seems to be the highest ideal. With "happiness" as the highest ideal for marriage, we'll lose the picture that marriage was created to display. And if happiness is your greatest pursuit, your commitment will easily give way when the going gets tough.

Yes, marriage, as God intends, will bring much happiness, rich joy, true fulfillment, and pleasure—but only when we enter marriage in the way the Designer planned. When we throw away God's design for marriage, and we chuck the purpose behind it, we begin our descent into confusion. God's design for marriage is being dismembered, as the purpose behind it has been lost.

A few years ago, I (Kim) witnessed a large mob of people demanding to be seen and heard. This very vocal group felt they were being treated unjustly, because in most states they couldn't receive legal standing as a "married couple." Signs shouting "Equal Treatment!" and "LOVE" were sprinkled through the crowd. But one sign stood out to me above the others. Someone had taken the liberty to drag Jesus into the mix and put their opinion on the sign as though it was Jesus' take on the topic.

The sign read: "Jesus is for Same-Sex Marriage." Really? Had Jesus conveyed that to this individual? How?

We don't know everything that Jesus said and did, but thankfully, Jesus did give us a definitive word on marriage that applies to this issue.

And Pharisees came up to him and tested him by asking, "Is it lawful to divorce one's wife for any cause?" He answered, "Have you not read that he who created them from the beginning made them male and female, and said, 'Therefore a man shall leave his father and his mother and hold fast to his wife, and the two shall become one flesh'? So they are no longer two but one flesh. What therefore God has joined together, let not man separate." (Matthew 19:3–6)

When the question of divorce came to the forefront, Jesus defined the marriage model by taking the group back to Genesis where we see God create, define, and establish the institution of marriage: "God created man in his own image, in the image of God he created him; male and female he created them" (Genesis 1:27).

God created two genders. Two. He repeats this distinction of two created genders in Genesis 5:2, reiterating the classification of "male and female." He created the prototypical couple, the first marriage, as our example—male and female—united by God: "Therefore a man shall leave his father and his mother and hold fast to his wife, and they shall become one flesh" (Genesis 2:24).

God does not mistakenly create a male body to house a "female spirit" or create "two spirited" people (as some ancient traditions promote) to house both male and female spirits within one body. God created male and female. Within those genders, individuals may have a variety of tendencies that are not stereotypical of their particular gender, but each individual is created by God as male or female.

It is obvious that many people (in increasing numbers) struggle with their gender identity. We should reach out and seek to help them, just as we should assist anyone who is struggling with any issue. We live in a fallen world where all individuals begin with a warped view of their personal identity, and to some extent we all struggle with types of "identity confusion."

But the truth is, we were created with gender and created for the purpose of displaying God's image to others: "Then God said, 'Let us make man in our image, after our likeness . . .'" (Genesis 1:26). That is our true identity.

Nothing else in creation is given this designation of being created in God's image. You, me, each individual, we are created in God's likeness, in His image . . . we're created to image God—to bear His reflection. We are created to bear His likeness through our gender and our gender plays a role in displaying the great mystery.

The great mystery is under attack when God's ordained structure for marriage is undermined. To understand the significance of the same-sex marriage debate, we must understand God's purpose for marriage. The display of two genders united in marriage provides a significant metaphor. God's design of marriage is the physical model He created to display His great mystery: the relationship between Jesus (the divine Bridegroom) and the church (His bride) as seen in Ephesians 5:22–33. The great mystery trumps our search for "personal happiness at any cost" every time.

Of all the metaphors God employs in describing His love relationship with us, the marriage metaphor seems to be His favorite; it flows freely throughout all of Scripture. The fact that marital love is the narrative arc of three Old Testament books (Ruth, Song of Songs, and Hosea) indicates the significance of this metaphor. In each of these beautiful portrayals, we see the picture of God's devoted and redemptive love.

We can see telling parallels in God's devotion to Israel and His purpose in the institution of marriage, but the most significant is the *nature* of the relationship; its nature is one of covenant. He is a covenant-keeping God and this knowledge brings comfort and the sense of belonging, but it also has huge implications when we apply it to the marriage relationship.[2]

Throughout the Old Testament, the magnitude of God's faithfulness stands in stark contrast to His bride's unfaithfulness. The book of Hosea in particular exposes the reader to the pain and anguish of the Almighty (through Hosea, the faithful husband), while at the same time showcasing God's unrelenting love and pursuit of His people (represented by Hosea's immoral wife, Gomer). Within this small book, the descriptive *hesed* is used six times.

The word חֶסֶד (*hesed* or *chesed*) in the Hebrew Bible is difficult to translate into English because, according to language scholars, it really has no precise equivalent in our language. I discovered the word when I was reading Hosea and a footnote grabbed my attention. I've never recovered from the impact of the words I read that day.

The footnote was in reference to Hosea 2:19–20 (NASB):

I will betroth you to Me forever;
>Yes, I will betroth you to Me in righteousness and in justice,
>In lovingkindness and in compassion,

And I will betroth you to Me in faithfulness.
>Then you will know the Lord.

The footnote described *hesed* as "loyal, steadfast, or faithful love and stresses the idea of a belonging together of those involved in the love relationship." In this particular verse the word is translated "lovingkindness" (NASB) and refers to "God's faithful love for His unfaithful people."[3]

The frequent use of the word, not only in Hosea but throughout Scripture, is significant. *Hesed* occurs 245 times in the Old Testament.[4] Perhaps no other word in all of Scripture so beautifully describes God's nature or vividly portrays His character. We see His heart most clearly when His actions demonstrate *hesed* through His covenant relationship with man.

> The obligations and rights acquired through a covenant are translated into corresponding actions through *hesed*. *Hesed* is the real essence of *berith* (Hebrew: covenant), and it can almost be said that it is its very content. The possibility of the origin and existence of a covenant was based on the existence of *hesed* . . . they are not to be understood as being entirely synonymous but as being mutually contingent upon one another.[5]

Covenant. It's more than halfhearted promises or good intentions. For God, it is a sacrificial commitment sealed by His own blood. It is sacred faithfulness forging through every obstacle to pursue His bride. It is Hosea going to the slave block to purchase his wayward wife out of prostitution.

That's you and me.

And God not letting us go—no matter how far we've run.

This marital covenant is graphically portrayed in Scripture as an intimate and personal love affair between God and His people. Although it's seen as a binding, legal agreement, the covenant relationship is not dry legalism. We feel God's deep emotion in the prophet's passages where he is lamenting the loss of the original love relationship. God is passionate in His commitment to His bride.

Hesed is what drives and seals God's covenant. In the New Testament, it is the essence of the gospel. An unrelenting God pursuing an undeserving sinner and paying an unbelievable ransom to purchase an unworthy and unfaithful bride. He spills valuable blood to secure our redemption and wraps us in His rich robes of righteousness, speaking words of safety, "You are mine now. All is well."

The Bridegroom

God designed the most intimate of all earthly relationships to serve as a real-life parable depicting His commitment to His bride. Marriage is God's platform displaying to the watching world a physical picture of a spiritual reality. Marriage is God's personal symbol and signature.

On the sixth day of creation God created man "in His own image." Adam was designed to serve as a *type*—a limited representation of the Almighty (Romans 5:14). The role of husband was designed to portray the eternal Bridegroom—who will return for His bride, the church—as typified by the wife (Ephesians 5:25–28).

According to Martin Luther and a host of biblical scholars, the nearest New Testament equivalent to *hesed* is grace.

Hesed: unfathomable grace providing the way to an uncommon communion—the redeemed sinner in fellowship with Holy God. A model of God as the "transcendent other" in relationship with mortal man.

Infinite wed to finite.

The beauty of *hesed* is seen in its most glorious form on a bloody cross as the Bridegroom pours out the atoning price to redeem His bride. But it is also seen in the final pages that record our future uniting with Him: when He comes for His bride as a returning Warrior-King wearing a robe dipped in blood.

> Then I heard what seemed to be the voice of a great multitude, like the roar of many waters and like the sound of mighty peals of thunder, crying out,
>
> Hallelujah!
> For the Lord our God the Almighty reigns. Let us rejoice and exult and give him the glory, for the marriage of the Lamb has come, and his Bride has made herself ready . . .

Then I saw heaven opened, and behold, a white horse! The one sitting on it is called Faithful and True, and in righteousness he judges and makes war. His eyes are like a flame of fire, and on his head are many diadems, and he has a name written that no one knows but himself. He is clothed in a robe dipped in blood, and the name by which he is called is The Word of God. (Revelation 19:6–7, 11–13)

When the world bombards you with messages like:

"You can do better—call it quits and move on . . ."

"What does it matter if it's a same-sex marriage—two people love each other—that's all that matters . . ."

"The heterosexual view of marriage is completely outdated . . ."

"Living together before marriage? It's no big deal!"

When you hear those statements—I hope you'll be reminded of the cross. I hope you'll take a good look at the Bridegroom as He pours out His lifeblood to redeem you. I hope you'll recognize that your marriage is to be a picture of that love. I hope you'll choose to live worthy of the Bridegroom's sacrifice. I hope it will inspire you to make a visible stand for the transcendent value of marriage.

Remember that "transcendent cause" that LeRoy challenged you to consider in the last chapter? This is that cause. The gospel is the transcendent cause that your marriage represents. This is why your marriage matters. This is why the battle is so serious. This is why we are crying out to defend marriage as God has defined it.

LeRoy and I are not opposed to same-sex marriage because of the individuals who demanded its legalization. We're not opposed because we're "homophobes" or hate-mongers or because we're trying to push people's buttons. We are opposed to same-sex marriage because it stands in direct opposition to God's revelation of Himself. We're opposed because it strips the marriage model from its ability to display the gospel.

Although some may claim that our opinion is merely an opinion, our stance is not rooted in any personal agenda, but is based on what God has clearly revealed through His Word—which is the highest authority. When someone attempts to speak for Jesus by placing "His opinion" on a placard, it is obvious that our culture is confused on where God stands on this issue. As believers, it is our responsibility to address the marriage topic and explain what God has stated. But, actions speak louder than words, and sadly, we believers have lost our voice.

The Church Has Lost Her Credibility

Sadly, the church is not standing in a strong position to speak on the same-sex marriage issue because we have failed to establish marriages that display the picture God intended. It is hypocritical of us to decry the moral failure in America without calling the church to repentance because of the condition of our marriages. The church's divorce rate does not bring God glory, and in fact, the condition of a high percentage of the church's marriages brings blasphemy to God's Word.

The church has lost its voice to speak credibly on this issue because the majority of the church's heterosexual marriages are not reflecting the power of the gospel.

We were guilty of this in our marriage.

I was guilty of this as a wife. I was "reviling" the Word of God by claiming to be a follower of Jesus Christ, but living with obvious resentment toward my husband. I claimed to love God but I was a shrew to live with. Our marriage did not display the love relationship that God intended for married couples to experience.

The beautiful description of marriage that Ephesians 5 gives is what God desires in the church. The model of the husband (representative of Christ) and the wife (representative of the church) is a picture of the love relationship that we are to display to others in our marriages. But that kind of marriage is only possible through the transformation provided by Christ's atoning work on the cross. It is only possible when two sinful mates apply the truth of God's Word through the empowering grace of the Holy Spirit.

I am deeply ashamed that for many years our marriage did not reflect the picture of the gospel, did not glorify God, or give credence to the power of His Word. Once God opened my eyes to what I was doing, it brought me to my knees, to lasting repentance, to a point of asking LeRoy's forgiveness and committing to surrender my will to God's Word.

Writing *Fierce Women* is the fruit of God's amazing work in our marriage and the book you hold in your hands is additional fruit. LeRoy and I share a deep and growing burden for marriages that are broken and hurting. We're asking God to meet with you in these pages, to comfort you, instruct you, and challenge you to lead your fierce woman to the throne of grace and begin to live out the marriage God has created for you to experience.

We are praying that those who don't know Christ will be impacted through marriages where husbands and wives live with one another in humility, demonstrating the love of Christ, submitting to the authority of His Word, and walking in the fruit of the Spirit. We're asking God to bring revival to the church and return her voice so that the church can credibly speak to the culture and win the hearts of a lost and needy world.

Will you join us? Will you consider the transcendent cause that your marriage represents and the implication of failing to provide a clear gospel picture through your marriage?

⧚ DIGGING IN ⧚

1. What does Revelation 19:6–16 describe? Who is on the white horse and what is He called? We began with a wedding in Genesis 3 and now Scripture is depicting how mankind's history on earth will be concluded—with another wedding. If you are a Christian, you will participate in this most significant event. How are you preparing now to spend eternity in this Bridegroom's presence?

2. In Matthew 25:14–30, Jesus gives a parable teaching the joy and reward that will be given to His faithful servants. Read through this passage, but focus on verse 23, and allow that to motivate you in your determination to glorify God through your marriage.

3. How can your marriage display the gospel? Why does that matter? How is your marriage impacting other family members, children, siblings, friends, your church, the culture?

On the Threshold of a Glorious Beginning

⟫◇⟪

*The Lamb's wedding is a time for boundless pleasure,
and tears would be out of place . . . God himself will dwell
among men; and surely at his right hand there are pleasures
for evermore, and tears can no longer flow.*[1]

CHARLES SPURGEON

P atrick took his last breath at thirty years old. He didn't plan to enter his "glorious beginning" that soon. But God's goodness extends beyond what we understand. The mystery of His goodness includes the eternal perspective that looks to the unseen with joy. True love doesn't hang onto our loved ones, but true love yearns for God's best for them, and that best includes their move to the eternal realm.

From my limited vantage point, it seems Patrick's life was far too short. We need more men like Patrick, more true men who lead their families to love Christ, who spiritually challenge and equip the men around them. But God's vantage point goes beyond mine.

Patrick's final day reflected how he'd lived his life. It was full. He loved others well and had his heart and mind fixed on eternity before he ever arrived there. He spent his last afternoon with a young man he'd been discipling, and during their time together they discussed the "end times." At one point, Patrick sat back, crossed his arms, and told the young man, "Hey, if God wants to take me, I'm ready." Less than twenty-four hours from that statement Patrick would be standing in the literal presence of his Savior—experiencing the adventures of heaven firsthand.

That Tuesday morning began like any other for Brittany, but within a few short hours of kissing her beloved Patrick good-bye as he left for work, she received a call that would rock her world forever. Without warning, Patrick's heart stopped. His beautiful wife's reaction to becoming a widow at twenty-five with three boys under the age of three, gives evidence that Patrick served her well as a spiritual leader, and his shepherding prepared her for navigating such a shocking loss. He prepared Brittany by pointing her to place her dependence on Christ rather than on himself. Brittany shared (by video) at the memorial service:

> In that moment, when my whole world rocked . . . God was faithful . . . eternity became so real. If there is anybody in this world that was ready to meet the Lord, it was Patrick, he walked so close and so deep with the Lord, and even in his death—he was challenging me to grow deeper in the Lord. Our prayer has always been that God would be magnified, and that God would be glorified in our lives, whatever it takes.
>
> My challenge to you is—you never know when you will meet and be faced with eternity. None of us knew that morning, his heart just stopped beating, there's no explanation . . . nothing but God . . . there's no guilt, there's no regret . . . he was ready. Of all the things in the

world, he would want you to know Jesus Christ. All of these things that we see, that we spend our mind and heart focused on is temporary . . . No matter where you are . . . you can live your life in the mundane, in the hard times, in the low times and do it with an eternal mindset.[2]

Patrick left behind his beloved Brittany and their three boys, grieving parents, sisters, and many family members. Left behind also are people who responded to the gospel message that Patrick lived out day by day. Many accepted Christ at his memorial service and now have assurance that they, too, will one day have their entrance into the glorious beginning that has no end.

At Patrick's service, one speaker stated: "Patrick Keith Price was a difference maker. He made the world a better place to be . . . he inspired me to be a better person."

Patrick was one of those men who leaves a "wake of goodness and mercy" in his path. Psalm 23:6 describes "goodness and mercy" following behind the life that God shepherds. Just as a boat moves across the waters of a lake, leaving a visible trail behind, your life is creating a wake.

We've all seen the negative version of this—friends or family members, cruising through life with no concern for anyone but themselves. What you see in the wake of their selfish lives is like the devastation of an EF-5 tornado ripping a thirty-mile swath across Oklahoma. Misery and the tragedy of wrecked lives lie strewn behind it like a human debris field.

But then there is the other life, the one you were created to live, the one that leaves the "goodness and mercy" wake behind it. God's kind intention and plan for your life, and your marriage, is for the "wake" of His great love to touch every life that your life touches. Think about it, an ever-widening, ever-expanding trail of God's goodness, God's mercy, God's glory spreading to every life that crosses your path. That is what God wants to do in your life and through your marriage.

At Patrick's memorial service, not only was his wife a visible testimony of Patrick's strong spiritual leadership, but there were dozens of young men—all wearing white shirts—who stood as a testament to Patrick's investment in their lives. At the end of the service, these white-shirted young men filed out of the church together, and it looked like an enormous wave of white—a wake of goodness and mercy—exiting the building.

Leaving the Wake of Goodness and Mercy

What does the "wake" of your life look like? How would others respond to your sudden exit from this realm? What would be left behind for others to see as tangible evidence of God's transforming power?

If I would have made my exit at the lowest point in our marriage, I would have left behind a wake of destruction and I would have missed all the good things God had in store. You may have picked up this book in a final desperate attempt because you've almost lost all hope. You dread the future. You are weary and have no desire to go on, because you believe every day is going to be like the one before. Things will never change. Even if there is a temporary reprieve, a return to the same misery is inevitable and things will likely grow worse.

I have lived more days like that than I can count. In those times of despair, I was convinced that there was no answer, no escape, and I gave up on any response from heaven. I felt like I was on my own. This was now my life. Depression was my new normal. All I could do was adjust and attempt to cope. Life was sheer misery.

But I was wrong. In those days, I had no clue how wrong I was.

Many of you know exactly what I'm talking about. You have been there. You may be there right now. You may not believe me, but you do not have to remain in hopeless misery. Believing that there is no hope for change is believing a lie. I believed the lie for years. Not any longer. I want to tell you what I believe now.

God has planned good for you and not evil. God's good may not always look like our good—but His good is always the *best good*. Allow me to remind you of a truth you already know. God is able to bring the best out of the worst. This is the way of our God.

Let's return to the passage for husbands and see the warning and promise of God. We get a glimpse into the mysterious and powerful dynamic of praying husbands in 1 Peter 3:7: "Likewise, husbands, live with your wives in an understanding way, showing honor to the woman . . . since they are heirs with you of the grace of life, so that your prayers may not be hindered." That warning of your prayers being "hindered" is followed with the promise of a love for life and seeing "good days":

"For whoever desires to love life and see good days, let him keep his tongue from evil and his lips from speaking deceit; let him turn away from evil and do good; let him seek peace and pursue it" (1 Peter 3:10–11).

Does that sound anything like what you're currently experiencing? A love for life and lots of good days? Or do you feel more like you've already passed the gate in Dante's *Inferno* that reads: "Abandon all hope ye who enter here."

> GOD'S GOOD MAY NOT ALWAYS LOOK LIKE OUR GOOD—BUT HIS GOOD IS ALWAYS THE BEST GOOD.

Hang on—hope is not lost. There is a promise that God has for you.

Peter's encouragement to husbands contains a wonderful promise that sadly so many never experience. When he speaks of "being heirs together of the grace of life" it is a message to believers who are struggling under great hardship (1 Peter 3:7 KJV). *You are struggling, but brother, there is a future grace for your marriage.* There are blessings yet to come that you cannot now know.

God has stored up blessings beyond your ability to comprehend—and they are for you. I want to urge you to not only press on, but also joyfully to embrace the future God has planned for you. You and your wife have a shared destiny of God's grace: "for to this you were called, that you may obtain a blessing" (1 Peter 3:9).

Did you catch that? You are called to receive a blessing, to be a blessing, to live a life of blessing. It is God's will for you "to love life and see good days." Does that interest you? Do you even believe it is possible? It may not seem plausible at this moment, but that is God's calling for you. It is what He desires for your future. It is what He wants for your marriage. It is what He is able to provide for you. This is not a "your best life now" theology. It is the straightforward, unvarnished truth of God.

Future Grace and Lasting Peace

A few verses later Peter shares the key to experiencing this promise: "in your hearts honor Christ the Lord as holy" (1 Peter 3:15). There it is: allow Jesus to sit enthroned as Sovereign King. This is the key, but within this key lies the requirement of faithful obedience in dark times. To set apart Christ as Lord in your life and marriage means trusting your future to Him. It equates to living for Christ today in a way that most blesses others in your life. It involves making the hard choices now that will pay huge dividends later. Some of those hard choices are lined out within the promise: "let him keep his tongue from evil and his lips from speaking deceit; let him turn away from evil and do good; let him seek peace and pursue it" (1 Peter 3:10–11).

Pursuing "peace" is what this book is all about. Pursuing peace with God and peace with your fierce woman. Rich, rewarding,

God-centered, God-supplied peace. We've shared with you action steps all along the way as we've walked this journey together, and taking those steps will be hard. But faithful obedience to your King is what is required to experience the future grace and the lasting peace that He offers for your marriage. It will require you to be the man, to take heroic action, and to move out in faith.

Pulling the Plug on Your Sinking Ship

When I was a kid, my family spent a lot of time on Beaver Lake in Northwest Arkansas. I learned to ski there; it's where I caught bluegill, crappie, and largemouth bass. I loved skiing across the lake with the motor wide open, the wake widening behind us. I would jump our wake and look for wakes from other boats to jump—the bigger the boat, the better the wake.

On one camping trip, it rained furiously all night. When we went down to the shore to take out the boat that morning, we found our small Chris-Craft within an inch of surrendering to the water and sinking to the bottom of the bay. I thought we would have to spend all morning miserably bailing water, but my dad had a plan—something I would never have thought of (and really didn't want to try). He told me to climb in first; then he carefully stepped into the almost submerged boat and started the engine. As Dad slowly motored out of the inlet and into deeper water, he told me what I needed to do. And his idea scared me to death, in fact, I was fairly sure we would both die.

My dad told me to reach under the water, at the back of the boat, and find the plug. I was barely able to do this without going completely under. With grave seriousness, he instructed me to wait until we reached top speed, and then—pull the plug! Now, I'm no skilled sailor, but pulling the plug on a sinking ship sounded like suicide to me.

Dad warned me to hold the plug near the hole because if the engine sputtered or died we were going down . . . fast. There was no margin for error. If his plan didn't work, we would drown. I thought the whole thing was a terrible idea, but did as I was told, and something amazing happened. When we hit max speed, I pulled the plug. We didn't take on more water—in fact, the vacuum caused by the propeller running through the lake sucked all the water out of the boat.

What I thought would surely kill me saved the boat and ended up as a fun afternoon of skiing. What I thought was a crazy idea was actually wisdom. My dad's plan terrified me and made zero sense, but it turned out that he knew best. He didn't explain to me how it was going to work; he just needed my full cooperation and trust.

Friend, don't miss the future grace God has for you. You cannot imagine all God has planned for you. There are incredible blessings you will forfeit if you cave to despair.

You may be convinced that you're drowning. But trust me, God has not failed you. He is freeing you. God has not forsaken you. He is drawing you near. God is not through with you. He is just starting. This is not . . . I repeat, this is not the end. It is a glorious beginning!

Your Father has a plan. You're not going this alone; He knows where you are and is completely aware of your need. He is providing you with instructions, but it may feel like He's asking you to pull the plug on your sinking ship! Trust me, He won't drown you and He is not setting you up for failure. He is inviting you into His glorious beginning for you.

> Thus says the Lord, who makes a way in the sea, a path in the mighty waters, "Remember not the former things, nor consider the things of old. Behold, I am doing a new thing; now it springs forth, do you not perceive it? I will make a way . . . for I give water in the wilderness, rivers in the desert, to give drink to my chosen people, the people whom I formed for myself that they might declare my praise" (Isaiah 43:16, 18–21).

Age, time, and God's grace afford the opportunity for me to look back on all that I would have missed had I checked out of our marriage years ago. For almost two decades now, Kim and I have enjoyed the sweetest times in our marriage, ministry, and spiritual lives. We wrestle together in prayer, serve on the battlefield of ministry together, worship, cry, and laugh together. We are enjoying and thanking God for the "grace of life" He's poured out on us.

I'm thrilled to have the privilege of being "Poppy" to Teagan, Roman, Esther, Phoenix, and Adalynn. I am "loving life" and spending many "good days" with these precious gifts from God. I shudder to think how life could have been so different. The fact that you are reading this book is part of the future grace God had in store. Kim and I are blown away that He would use our misery, failures, and sin for His glory. If you would have told us in our darkest days that God would use the pain for great good, we could not have comprehended it.

In my darkest days, I had a crisis of faith, wondered if God was even there, but now I know that not only was He there, but He was doing an incredible work in the pain. If you knew all that God was doing, if you could see His ending from your beginning, I believe there would be nothing in His plan that you would change.

Imagine Your New Beginning

Brother, you might feel like you are out in the deepest part of the lake roaring along with the plug out. You see no way that this is going to work. Let me remind you that the Father's hands are on the wheel. He knows what He is doing. His work is often on a need-to-know basis and you do not need to know everything. Trust what He is doing. Trust the unknown and the unknowable to Him.

There is much that is hidden in mystery, but what we do know is that God has orchestrated a great redemptive plan and you are part of that. His plan for your life is to fill the earth with God's glory.

Fulfilling that mission begins with loving God more than you love yourself, and out of the overflow of your love relationship with Him—loving others. Your wife is to be the first recipient of that overflow of love. Only God can do that work—ask Him to provide the grace for courage to love your wife well and serve her as the spiritual leader God created you to be.

Kim and I share a dream that I want to share with you. Imagine with me what would happen if God were to capture men's and women's hearts for His glory. If by His Spirit's empowerment and grace, couples began to apply the truth of God's Word to their marriages, can you imagine what that would look like? What would happen if the transforming power of the gospel were seen in your marriage and through the marriage of every Christian couple that you know? What would happen if men of God began to rise up and lead their families?

What if godly husbands challenged their wives and children to love God more than they love themselves? What if God stirred the heart of every man who reads this book and raised up an army of servant warriors who would tenderly lead their wives to follow Christ daily? What would happen if the gospel could shine through the marriages within Christ's church?

Patrick lived the gospel and entered his eternal glorious beginning at only thirty. You have the opportunity today to step into the glorious beginning that God has for your marriage. It isn't too late. Trust me, I've experienced it—God is able to accomplish more than what you can now comprehend.

Are you ready to step into those grace-filled "good days"?

This is what He has for you:

"Now to him who is able to do far more abundantly than all that we ask or think, according to the power at work within us, to him be glory in the church and in Christ Jesus throughout all generations, forever and ever. Amen" (Ephesians 3:20–21).

⊰ DIGGING IN ⊱

1. Preparing for transitions requires a willingness to step into the unknown. You've experienced the heartache of a marriage without joy. Our hope is that you and your wife will enter the glorious beginning of the grace-filled future that He has for you. Jesus prayed for you in the last hours before His crucifixion as He was preparing His followers for the transition they would experience by His return to the Father. Read through Jesus' prayer in John 17 and realize that you and your wife are included in His request.

2. What desires does Jesus express in this prayer? How do these desires parallel the desires you have for your marriage? How can you apply this passage of Scripture to your prayers for your wife?

3. See God's heart for your marriage in Jeremiah 29:11. Do you believe God can bring transformation? Press forward into His glorious beginning for your marriage in the confidence that He is able.

Notes

Chapter 1: The Courageous Leader Within

1. Tom Chiarella, "What is a Man?," *Esquire*, March 1, 2015, http://www.esquire.com/lifestyle/a22462/what-is-a-man-0509/.

2. Matthew Henry, *Matthew Henry's Commentary on the Whole Bible*, vol. 1 (Peabody, MA: Hendrickson Publishers, 1991), 16.

3. Kimberly Wagner, *Fierce Women: The Power of a Soft Warrior* (Chicago: Moody Publishers, 2012), 19.

4. Oliver North, *American Heroes in Special Operations* (Nashville: B&H Publishing Group, 2010), 151.

Chapter 2: The Passive Deserter

1. C. S. Lewis, *The Four Loves*, as found in *The Inspirational Writings of C. S. Lewis* (Nashville: Thomas Nelson, 2004), 278–79.

2. "Clint Miller" is an amalgamation of many men I've talked with over the years. I've observed the devastation caused by the selfishness of countless numbers of men who truly believe they are justified, even living out "God's will" by leaving their family for a woman they "love."

3. Kimberly Wagner, *Fierce Women: The Power of a Soft Warrior* (Chicago: Moody Publishers, 2012), 40.

4. Albert Mohler, "Ashley Madison and the Death of Monogamy," Albert Mohler (blog), August 8, 2015, http://www.albertmohler.com/2015/08/27/ashley-madison-and-the-death-of-monogamy/.

Chapter 3: Anything You Can Do, She Can Do Better!

1. Kathleen Parker, "A Woman on Men: What Feminists Don't Seem to Get," *Houston Chronicle*, November 3, 2005, http://www.chron.com/opinion/outlook/article/Parker-A-woman-on-men-What-feminists-don-t-seem-1498983.php.

2. J. I. Packer, *Weakness Is the Way* (Wheaton, IL: Crossway, 2013), 14.

3. Albert Mohler, "From Boy to Man, the Marks of Manhood, Part One," Albert Mohler (blog), April 21, 2005, http://www.albertmohler.com/2005/04/21/from-boy-to-man-the-marks-of-manhood-part-one/.

4. Sarah Womack, "Modern Men Feel Emasculated," *The Telegraph*, March 26, 2008, http://www.telegraph.co.uk/news/uknews/1582863/Modern-men-feel-emasculated-study-claims.html.

5. John MacArthur, *The MacArthur Study Bible* (Nashville: Thomas Nelson, 2006), 1791.

6. Kimberly Wagner, *Fierce Women: The Power of a Soft Warrior* (Chicago: Moody Publishers, 2012), 57–58.

7. Womack, "Modern Men Feel Emasculated."

8. Janice Shaw Crouse, "Feminism, Marriage, and the Perpetually Adolescent Male," *Washington Times*, February 3, 2015, http://www.washingtontimes.com/news/2015/feb/3/janice-shaw-crouse-feminism-marriage-and-perpetual/?page=all.

9. Ibid.

10. Theodore Roosevelt, "Citizenship in a Republic" (speech, Sorbonne, Paris, France, April 23, 1910).

Chapter 4: Trapped in the Hurt Locker

1. Winston Churchill, quoted in Dennis Rainey, *Stepping Up: A Call to Courageous Manhood* (Little Rock: Family Life Publishing, 2011), 27.

2. Nancy Leigh DeMoss, *Biblical Portrait of Womanhood* (Buchanan, MI: Life Action Ministries, 1999), 9, 12, 13.

3. Nancy Leigh DeMoss, *Choosing Gratitude: Your Journey to Joy* (Chicago: Moody Publishers, 2009), 84.

4 Kimberly Wagner, *Fierce Women: The Power of a Soft Warrior* (Chicago: Moody Publishers, 2012), 82–83.

Chapter 5: Run into the Battle

1. Bernard Law Montgomery, AZQuotes.com, http://www.azquotes.com/quote/203767.

2. C. S. Lewis, *The Four Loves*, as found in *The Inspirational Writings of C. S. Lewis* (Nashville: Thomas Nelson Publishers, 2004), 278–279.

3. Colossians 3:12–21 is what we refer to as the "relationship template" for families. We encourage you to use this passage as a devotional study. Walk slowly through this passage (maybe nightly) and investigate meanings of words as well as talk about practical ways that these instructions can be applied to your relationship.

Chapter 6: What Your Wife Needs Most

1. John Piper, "Lionhearted and Lamblike: The Christian Husband as Head, Part 2: What Does It Mean to Lead" (sermon), Desiring God, March 25, 2007, http://www.desiring God.org/messages/lionhearted-and-lamblike-the-christian-husband-as-head-part-2.

Chapter 7: God's Got This!

1. Dietrich Bonhoeffer, *London: 1933–1935*, vol. 13, *Dietrich Bonhoeffer Works*, ed. Keith Clements, trans. Isabel Best (New York: Fortress Press, 2007), 308–09, quoted in Eric Metaxas, *Bonhoeffer: Pastor, Martyr, Prophet, Spy* (Nashville: Thomas Nelson, 2010), 241.

Chapter 8: How She Wants You to Love Her

1. Timothy Keller, *Prayer: Experiencing Awe and Intimacy with God* (New York: Penguin Group, 2014), 194.

2. Complementarism affirms that both men and women are created with equal worth and value, but recognizes gender role distinctions. The egalitarian view does not recognize role distinctions. This is an oversimplified explanation; for further research see: *Recovering Biblical Manhood and Womanhood: A Response to Evangelical Feminism*, ed. John Piper and Wayne Grudem (Wheaton, IL: Crossway Books, 1991).

3. Wayne Grudem, foreword to *Radical Womanhood: Feminine Faith in a Feminist World*, by Carolyn McCulley (Chicago: Moody Publishers, 2008), 11.

4. Ibid.

Chapter 9: Man to Man

1. A. W. Tozer, *Mornings with Tozer* (Chicago: Moody Publishers, 1991, 2008), January 3 entry.

Chapter 10: Never Go AWOL

1. Theodore Roosevelt, "The Strenuous Life, A Speech before the Hamilton Club" (speech, Chicago, April 10, 1899).

2. C. S. Lewis, *The Problem of Pain* (New York: Harper, 2001), 91.

3. Stephen Mansfield, *Mansfield's Book of Manly Men: An Utterly Invigorating Guide to Being Your Most Masculine Self* (Nashville: Nelson Books, 2013), xviii.

4. I've taken literary liberty, expanding Shammah's story beyond the details of 2 Samuel 23:8–12.

5. Sammy Tippit relayed this story to us in personal conversation and publicly through his ministry newsletter.

Chapter 11: What's the Big Deal about Marriage, Anyway?

1. Hershael York, "Is your marriage a picture of the gospel?" (blog), The Southern Blog, February 5, 2015, http://www.sbts.edu/blogs/2015/02/05/is-your-marriage-a-picture-of-the-gospel/.

2. Portions of this chapter are excerpts from Kimberly Wagner, *Fierce Women: The Power of a Soft Warrior* (Chicago: Moody Publishers, 2012), chapter 11.

3. Charles Caldwell Ryrie, *Ryrie Study Bible* (Chicago: Moody Press, 1995), 1378.

4. H. J. Zobel, Griefswald, *Theological Dictionary of the Old Testament*, vol. 5, ed. G. Johannes Botterweck and Helmer Ringgren, 5:44–64.

5. Nelson Glueck, *Hesed in The Bible*, (Cincinnati: The Hebrew Union College Press, 1967), 47.

Chapter 12: On the Threshold of a Glorious Beginning

1. C. H. Spurgeon, *Cheque Book of the Bank of Faith* (Fearn, UK: Christian Focus Publications, 1996), 28.

2. You can view Brittany sharing their story here: https://www.youtube.com/watch?v=nCu4h7-BUFU.

Guidelines When Confrontation Is Necessary

1. If your wife is plagued by a long-term pattern of sin, your responsibility as her brother in Christ, as her friend, and as her spiritual leader, is to come alongside her and bring gentle confrontation (see Proverbs 27:5–6; Galatians 6:1–2; and Matthew 18:15). Your natural inclination will be to run rather than to confront, but that is not demonstrating true love to your wife. Before confronting her, seek the Lord first. Spend time in prayer and the Word seeking direction and timing before holding this conversation (James 1:19–20).

2. Be sure your desire to confront stems from right motives—spiritual restoration for your wife and love for her as your sister in Christ—not in order to "fix things" more to your liking (Romans 12; 1 Thessalonians 5:14–15; Hebrews 12:14–15).

3. Search your own heart first—is there anything in your own life that you need to confess to God or your wife (Matthew 7:3–5)?

If you have unresolved sin issues, you need to deal with those before confronting anyone.

4. If you and your wife have been operating more like enemies, be prepared for an unpleasant reaction from her, but keep reminding yourself that your motive is not to gain her praise but is to care for her soul. Don't approach her with a pious, holier-than-thou attitude and expect to be heard. God opposes that kind of heart (1 Peter 5:5). It will be difficult, but be courageous and kind. Approach her with grace, humility, tenderness, and love (Ephesians 3:17; 4:31–32).

5. Consider writing out your concerns first before talking with your wife. Prepare yourself for this conversation by carefully covering the details without using language that could be inflammatory or hurtful.

6. Before confronting, release unrealistic expectations. Depend on the Holy Spirit to bring conviction, not your words. Resolve in your heart that this work is the Lord's.

7. Begin your conversation by communicating your appreciation for your wife, your love for her, and your desire to serve as a friend and companion in her journey of spiritual growth. Share your concerns in an honest but gracious manner—not accusing or placing blame. Let your wife know specifically why you need to talk about this concern. Ask her how you can serve her by being a spiritual leader to her and fulfilling your responsibility as her brother in Christ. Look together at Galatians 6:1–2.

8. Do not speak in anger, raise your voice, or become emotional or accusatory when bringing your concerns. If your wife reacts in those ways, stay the course, and ask God for grace to not be

intimidated by her reaction. If the situation becomes volatile, let your wife know that you want to have this conversation, and lay out the parameters for holding it without sinful emotional outbursts. Lead her in prayer, firmly and tenderly guide her heart to a calm place to discuss the issue. If it becomes apparent that this conversation cannot be held calmly (at this time), relay your concerns in written form and allow her time to process what you share.

9. Diligently, specifically, and regularly intercede in prayer for God to work as you wait for your wife's response to your confrontation. Pray from a hopeful and confident position—but not one that is demanding. Give her time and space.

10. If your wife remains unrepentant in sin and that sin reaches a level that requires the intervention of spiritual leadership, you will need to follow the process of confrontation as outlined in Matthew 18:15–18. Let her know your plans to do this and give additional time for God to work after sharing this passage with her.

Allow your wife to reap the consequences of her sin. She is responsible before God for her actions. No matter how difficult it is for you to watch—don't bail her out. God can use this time of humility and brokenness to bring her to a needed place of repentance.

GUIDELINES FOR RESTORATION

If you have violated your wife through viewing porn, or being unfaithful to her in any way, whether it's through flirtation with another woman or it has moved beyond that, you have betrayed her as her husband and protector. If your wife is unaware of this, it doesn't change the fact that you've sinned against her and against God.

Repentance Is Necessary

Your process of recovery must begin with repentance. It is necessary for you to recognize the gravity of sinning against God and your wife. Spend some time reading and praying through these Psalms: 32, 36, and 51. Seek God for grace to repent fully from your sin. Your repentance must be evident for recovery to begin. In the early stages of turning back to God, you will need to confess your sin to the appropriate people and, once you begin that process, you will experience painful consequences as a result of your sin. This will be hard, but it will actually aid you in recognizing the seriousness of your sin. Do not take shortcuts or attempt to escape the blows of those consequences; they will actually benefit you in the long run.

Deal with Unconfessed Sin

If you've sinned against your wife, and hidden your sin, it will remain a wall between you until you come clean with her. You've placed her in a vulnerable position by allowing your sin to become a spiritual stronghold in your marriage. If you want the darkness to lose its power, turn on the light. Darkness is where we enjoy hiding when we're attracted to sin's offerings (John 3:19–21) and getting into the light is the first step out of your cycle of slavery to sin (1 John 1:5–10). Getting into the light means confessing your sin, first to God and then to the appropriate people: if you've sinned against your wife, you need to confess your sin to her, if you've sinned against your church family, confess your sin to your church family.

If your sin has continued for a long period of time, or has the potential to bring devastating consequences when revealed, you may need to ask your pastor or a spiritually mature friend to assist you in approaching your wife to confess your sin to her. Recognize the gravity of your sin and don't expect your wife to immediately offer forgiveness. Your confession is just the first step down a very long road. Be patient with your wife and understand that she will be grappling with several emotions. You've injured her deeply. She will struggle with insecurity, rejection, body-image issues, jealousy, and painful suspicions. She may experience intense and horrific nightmares as a result of your infidelity. She needs your reassurance that you are committed to caring for her through this process.

Ask for Accountability

Seek out mature spiritual leaders in your church and ask them for help. Share your need with them and ask them to hold you accountable, to pour truth into your life, to provide spiritual counsel, and to help you in your recovery process. Depending on the level of deception and length of time involved in the sin, appropriate measures should be taken for accountability. This may include involving professional counselors and ministries who specialize in a particular area of addiction (we recommend Pure Life Ministries at: purelifeministries.org). If that isn't necessary, see if your church can provide some type of regular counseling. A network of mature believers who know about your vulnerabilities need to serve in this process. This is especially important in the early stages, but never assume you are "in the clear" and no longer need accountability. The accountability will lessen as trustworthiness is established over time, but all believers need to live with some type of accountability in place.

Shut Every Door

Don't leave any room to return to your sinful addiction. You may need to take drastic actions (Matthew 18:8–9). If you've had an affair with someone at your job, you need to relocate or establish boundaries where you will no longer have contact with that person. If necessary, delete social media accounts, change your phone number and email address. Do whatever is necessary to cut off open access to anyone you've been sinfully involved with to any degree.

If you've been involved with someone and haven't ended that relationship, contact them by phone in your wife's presence, let them know your wife is with you, and end the relationship immediately. Make it clear to them that you do not want to have any further contact with them.

Saturate Yourself with Truth

The only hope for full recovery is a fresh and serious commitment to God's Word. Sin's power over us is the result of losing our love for the Savior. The way we fuel our love is to grow in our understanding of who He is, to reach increasing levels of intimacy with Him, to come to a greater appreciation of the cross, grace, and His love. That will not happen apart from feeding on His Word.

Love Is Your Protection

You cannot break out of the cycle of sin on your own. You can try to clean yourself up, try to "turn over a new leaf," try to establish new habits . . . and those efforts may bring some temporary improvements. But the only thing that will bring complete transformation and lasting change is a new love relationship. Love for God provides the motivation to turn from sin when temptation offers its pleasures. As your love for God increases, your pleasure in Him will destroy temptation's pull on your heart. Ask the Spirit to fill you with love for God.

CHARACTERISTICS CONTRAST:

The Courageous Leader and the Passive Deserter

CHARACTERISTICS OF THE COURAGEOUS LEADER	CHARACTERISTICS OF THE PASSIVE DESERTER
1. In strength and dignity he bears the image of God and his deepest identity is found in his relationship with Christ.	His identity is shaped by his failures and weaknesses.
2. He fears God alone. His love for God is the motive that allows him to lead well.	Fear drives most of his decisions and actions. Often he is a people pleaser and wants to be well liked. He lives from the motive of getting love rather than living from the motive of loving God and others.
3. He knows his assignment and lives to accomplish it.	Passivity is his default position. He is too crippled by fear, insecurity, and the belief that he can't do anything right to attempt to tackle any leadership responsibility.
4. When faced with overwhelming obstacles and daunting challenges, he pushes past the pain and trusts in his God.	Past failures often prevent him from persevering when faced with challenges and obstacles.
5. He accepts the mantle of leadership that God has placed upon him, seeing it not as a burden, but a privilege.	The guilt of deserting his leadership post becomes an oppressive burden and pressure that saps him of strength, confidence, and hope.
6. He knows that his strength lies solely in his humility before God and his complete dependence on Christ.	He operates in weakness because he is depending on his own strength, independent from God.
7. He is not ashamed to love with passion, conviction, and sacrifice.	He is too defeated to live or love passionately.
8. If required, he willingly lays down his life for his God, God's truth, his wife, his children, or anyone else who should need a defender or rescuer.	He reacts to painful circumstances and conflict by running or hiding in order to protect himself.

CHARACTERISTICS OF THE COURAGEOUS LEADER	CHARACTERISTICS OF THE PASSIVE DESERTER
9. He is generous with all he has, regretting only that he does not have more to give.	He hoards what he has, living in the mode of self-protection.
10. While others may wither, complain, or retreat in the storms of battle, trial, and affliction—by God's grace he is the warrior that continues to stand.	He is no warrior; he withers, complains, or retreats in the storms of battle.
11. He is known as a man of his word.	He tends to exaggerate, excuse, self-justify, and will even lie if necessary, in order to protect himself from painful consequences. You cannot depend on what he says.
12. He is known by his strength of character, and his tenderness of heart.	Sarcasm, insulting statements, and rude behavior are used to mask his spiritual weakness. His self-focus prevents compassion or tenderness.
13. He wears the mantle of a prophet with conviction and courage but with a heart to administer grace to the listener.	He is too insecure to speak truth in love. His self-absorption with his own "perceived injuries" prevents him from being able to come alongside others who are in need of healing and grace.
14. As a recipient of God's grace and forgiveness, he freely extends God's grace and forgiveness to others.	He relishes the role of victim; he believes he is "owed an apology" and therefore is unable to extend grace and forgiveness. He is unaware or unappreciative of God's grace that has been demonstrated to him.
15. His singular purpose is to glorify God.	His singular purpose is to protect himself.

Appreciation

---◆---

Thank you, Greg Thornton, for being the first to approach me with the idea of putting our story in book form, which resulted in *Fierce Women* being published. Your encouragement, and especially the prayers you and Grace have faithfully lifted to the throne for us, our family, and our latest writing endeavor, have been a great treasure to us personally.

Thank you, Rachel, Adam, Caleb, and Lindsey—for your patience, support, and encouragement as we plowed our way through this project!

Thank you, precious friend Jeanne Pender, for preparing a home-cooked meal for us every Thursday night through this project. Whenever we were exhausted and weary, we remembered that Thursday was coming, and we'd get a much-needed recharge. You knew we needed the nourishment and fellowship—so grateful for you!

Thank you, dear sisterhood, for your faithful prayer support and encouragement all along the way! You are a precious gift: Nancy DeMoss Wolgemuth, Holly Elliff, Mary Ann Lepine, Jennifer Lyell, Carolyn McCulley, Mary Kassian, and Dannah Gresh.

We are grateful for each who read, gave input, and especially prayed for the writing of the book: Lindsey Wagner, Jason and Annette Melton, Becky Arnold, Vivian Etherington, and Brian Kunkel. Your encouragement breathed strength into us!

Thank you, dear Dayspring Family, for your loving support

through the writing of the book and for your desire for God to spread our story to other hurting couples. Thank you for praying specifically and faithfully for us all along the way.

We appreciate the faithful blog readers at kimberlywagner.org who sent many words of encouragement and prayer—you all were an integral part of this process and walked with us through the entire journey—thank you!

Thank you, precious Judy Dunagan—what a joy you've been. Thank you for your belief in this project from the very beginning. For placing that call at such a providential time to invite us to consider writing this book! Thank you for supporting us during our recordings at "Focus on the Family" and praying for this all along the way. Moody is blessed to have you serving their authors—you are the fragrance of Christ.

Thank you, Betsey Newenhuyse, for your many words of encouragement and for applying your editing skills in a thoughtful and insightful manner. Thank you for being gracious with our enormous word count! You were a good and kind editor.

And finally, thank you, Nancy and Revive Our Hearts Ministries, for encouraging us to share our story, first in a Revive Our Hearts newsletter, then on radio, and finally through producing a video that has been used for the kingdom's sake beyond what we could have imagined.

About the Authors

LeRoy Wagner has served as a pastor and speaker for more than thirty years. His greatest desire is to see God's glory fill the earth, and he believes that begins with training individuals to live out the gospel in their homes and through their daily life experiences. The supreme love of his life is Jesus Christ; then his wife, Kimberly, and their children and grandchildren.

Kimberly Wagner's deepest passion is to spread God's glory. You can read Kim's daily blog at www.kimberlywagner.org, where she encourages women to be students of the Word. Kim is the author of *Fierce Women: The Power of a Soft Warrior* and a frequent guest on the *Revive Our Hearts* radio program, as well as a regular contributor to the True Woman blog. She is an author, a women's conference speaker, and a blogger.

I believe this account of Kimberly's journey and the truths
God used to change her heart and restore her marriage
will minister much grace and help to other "fierce women."
Nancy DeMoss Wolgemuth,
author, host of *Revive Our Hearts* radio

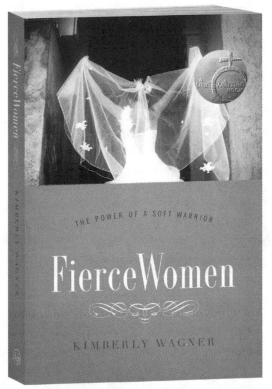

ISBN-13: 978-0-8024-0620-0

No matter whether you're an extrovert or more
introverted, Kimberly Wagner believes women are created
to be a compelling force.

You may not see yourself as beautifully fierce or even
slightly strong, but what if God has placed a powerful
fierceness within you—within every woman?

MOODY
Publishers™

From the Word to Life
www.MoodyPublishers.com